Where Did All The Money Go?
& *other* stories

by **Paul Schiernecker**

© Paul Schiernecker

Cover art by Adam Gardner

Dear Friend,

What follows is a collection of short stories about university life and experiences. I would like to express the stories contained mainly follow periods of downtime from studying. It wasn't all like this. There were sleepless nights spent high on caffeine trying to meet deadlines, there were worrying trips to the clinic and there were some days when I wondered if I had made completely the wrong choice and should have stuck it out at Sainsburys because I am sure I could have been the team leader of the Provisions department by now.

*These ten stories are for the most part things that happened to me. You should therefore be able to spot the same thinly veiled version of myself repeated through different stories but alongside that are tales I was either present for or heard about from those directly involved. I have tried to change as many of the names as possible and feel obliged to state these are just **my** views. This is just my experience, my perception of what I saw and what took place. I may be rose-tinting it, I may be shit-tinting it, but it's in print now and I refuse to apologise.*

Thank you for your time and money

Paul Schiernecker

For **Jocasta**

Contents

Best Man	1
Home	17
Amsterdam	37
The Devillenerve Sisters	64
The Curse Of Iggy Sutcliffe	79
The Night Of The Fridge Graveyard	92
Madcat On The Prowl	111
Monopoly	128
Where Did All The Money Go?	147
I Now Pronounce You	161

Best Man

MICHAEL
February 2010

It was one of those occasions Oliver would invariably refer to as my '8 Mile moments', the little pocket of time before anything was expected of me when I would bolt for the toilet to shit, be sick or just sweat it out and stare myself down in the mirror. Oliver couldn't make it down and I really could have done with him being there. This was a big one. It was different to playing guitar. It was different to being up in front of two hundred people and singing, as I had done before with the minimal amount of strain on my nerves. I had to talk. I had to entertain. I had to be amusing and I didn't have a guitar between myself and my audience.

I tugged at the awkward piece of ivy cloth at my neck classified by everyone else as a cravat. It felt as though it were tightening on me, restricting my airway and speech delivering abilities. I checked the pockets of my hired suit jacket one at a time to make sure I had everything I needed. I ran my fingers around the shape of the box of twenty Marlboro Lights, which was in my left hip pocket while the right housed the pocket watch Harry had given me that morning as a present. I had managed to abstain from smoking through the whole day just as I had promised to do, but it was all I could think of. My addiction tapped me on the shoulder at five-minute intervals. I wanted to disappear outside for a bit and smoke maybe one, or two, or the whole pack, just to put off the inevitable. It wasn't to be though. I had to go and face the music.

I checked myself over in the mirror for what must have been the fiftieth time that day. There was fear hidden in the depths of each of my grey eyes despite the glaze early afternoon drinking had caused them. The fresh cut of my hair still looked alien to me. I had gone from a mushroom of curls to what was ostensibly known at the time as the 'New London Haircut'. It looked more eighties than new on me, and it didn't look right. At least I could pass it off as being part of my shtick. I bared my teeth at my own reflection to try and look tough, as though I could hold dominion, but all I noticed was the pink gloss of a whole bottle of wine coating my teeth, gums and tongue. I hadn't really thought about it at the time. My problem is if someone puts a bottle of red down in front of me I will instinctively drink the whole thing, as quickly as possible, regardless of the etiquette the event should be afforded. I had purposely avoided the queue of people checking the seating plan because I didn't need it. I knew exactly where I was sitting and I made sure there was a bottle of wine there as soon as I was seated. I took every available moment after that to inhale it.

I tried to brush my hair over to one side to lessen the impact it had sitting heavily between my eyebrows but it refused to comply and just flopped back, making me look like Tony Hadley. Suddenly I reached a personal limit. The self-deprecating bit can only go on for so long before you realise it is all just inevitable. With a deep breath I threw myself backwards from where I had been leaning heavily on the sink. I walked out of the toilet altogether in fact, across the laminated dance floor, between the circular tables of wedding guests, and then took my seat at the top table.

John, or the father of the bride, as he would be known for the duration of the day turned and checked me over.

'You alright there Mikey? You look a bit green'. He launched back on his chair laughing. 'If you want I don't mind reading your speech. We can just say you're feeling a bit under the weather or something'.

'I'm fine John' I replied. 'I just get a bit nervous. I'll be fine. Thanks'. Those were the last words I said for a while. I felt I needed to try and preserve my voice, in the way a diva will refuse to speak to anyone during the day preceding a big show.

With dinner out of the way the general volume in the room had increased. I looked over to where my parents were sat, talking to another couple they had only met that day. I assumed they were discussing me. Suddenly the room was entirely hushed by the sound of several teaspoons chinking against several wine glasses. Harry stood to address them all. We were wearing similar suits and while mine felt as though it had been hired for a man twice my width Harry looked every shade of dapper in his. I couldn't help but feel this was a conscious decision by the tailor to make Harry look better than me on his wedding day. His speech was brilliant, considering we had sat down with a bottle of whiskey the night before to write it. Suddenly it was over and he passed the attention of the room over to me.

'Now ladies and gentlemen, a few polite words from my best mate and best man, Michael'. He looked cautiously over at me as the room was filled with another round of applause. His gaze said so much to me. In that moment he wished he had read my speech over properly, or even offered to write it for me. He wished he had told the staff to keep the wine away from the top table until the speeches were out of the way. Most of all he hoped I wasn't going to vomit there and then.

I slowly took to my feet as the cheers died away. I looked down at the leaf of A4 paper folded into a quarter, which had somehow found its way into my hand. It looked slightly used from where I had repeatedly withdrawn it from my suit jacket, checked it over and returned it, making sure I could remove a piece of paper from my pocket when under pressure. I thought I was a cowboy, practicing his quick draw. It had never been a concern I had encountered before, and yet as I lifted it up as though it were a newborn bird fallen from the nest it felt as though I had never handled anything so precious in my life. I felt I could crush the life from it with my bare hands. I opened it with the caution of a bomb disposal expert and then looked up, not at anyone in particular but focusing on a single point at the back of the room. Everything fell completely silent like the moment before a high impact crash and in the peace of it all I drifted back four and a half years.

****

'Put it on Mike. Put it on now. It'll be funny. We need to see it before the big night'. I hated being called 'Mike' but it was one of those awkward situations where you couldn't really chastise anyone because they always seemed to be doing it with the best of intentions. They always think they are being chummy and regular, that it is a sign of how well everyone is getting along. It didn't work. I wasn't a Mike. I always wanted to be a Mike but it is just not in my character. I will never be a Mike. The 'big night' being referred to was Halloween, a day devoid of importance after the age of ten that suddenly reared it's fake blood smeared head again at sixteen with the idea of eggings, drunken parties and slutty cat and witch costumes. It was two days before Halloween, which fell on a Wednesday that year. This was apparently a big deal on campus because Wednesday was *the* night out for the boys of the football team.

Through no fault of my own I had found myself living in Halls of Residence on the St Christopher's side of campus with one of the real big players of the football team. Our campus was split into two sets of accommodation, one on either side of the road where the Student's Union, refectory and lecture theatres were based. St Christopher's was for the more affluent students. My parents had kindly paid my accommodation fees and because it was my first year thought it would be best to damn the expense and rent me a room with an en suite bathroom. The flats in St Christopher's were shared between five while those in St John's were shared between eight or nine but were considerably cheaper.

I had promised to not only attend the party but to do so wearing the only fancy dress costume I had brought with me from home under the assumption it would be hilarious. The costume was a Spider-Man outfit built for eight to ten year olds. I was eighteen, six foot tall and built like a worn rake. While I am sure it was amusing to behold it played havoc with the enjoyment of the sensation in my extremities. The elasticised cuffs were so tight my hands and feet went slightly blue whenever I wore it for an extended period of time.

'Go on Mike' someone repeated, 'it'll be a laugh!'

In order to stop them from asking and purely for the sake of my own peace and sanity I disappeared off into my room and put the costume on. When I returned to the kitchen I was met with howls of laughter. I hadn't even bothered to put the mask on and already I felt like a right muppet.

'Go and run around campus' someone suggested.

'No!' I finally managed to will myself to say, despite the fact it had already gone too far.

'Go on, it'll be funny'.

If I had a pound for every time I have done something simply because somebody said 'it'll be funny' I would probably have the money to afford to sit down with a therapist and take a good long hard look at exactly why I metaphorically bend over to requests worded in this fashion. I assume it has something to do with wanting to have sex with my mother. Therapists always think it is something to do with wanting to have sex with your mother.

And so it was I took to the streets of campus in a child's fancy dress costume and my dirty white Adidas trainers 'for a laugh'. The funny thing about it was once I started jogging I actually enjoyed it. I ran along the edge of our building, past lit up bedroom windows and then headed into the centre. The flats in St Christopher's Quads were arranged rather tellingly in a square, with a patch of grass in the centre intersected from the corners by a path, which met in the middle as a cross where a single streetlight stood. I knew by running through the centre I would be seen, if not by late night revellers sitting on the slope drinking and smoking then by people sat in the comfort of their flats watching TV. They couldn't help but pay attention to any movement in their precious quad. I heard woops and catcalls from my flatmates as I ran through the centre. Catching sight of myself in a blacked out window as I ran under the light I couldn't help but laugh, it did look funny. After passing through the quad and getting some attention I decided to milk it in the way I had done since childhood and as I would continue to do.

Just milk this mildly amusing thing until that teat is good and dry, there's a good lad my subconscious always seemed to be saying.

From the far side of our block I ran down the path, under another streetlight and across what I assume had once been a river but was by then just a slight dip in the path covered in pebbles. This route led to the other blocks of flats, known as the Courts. As I was running the external circumference I heard someone scream for me, well, not for me, but for my hooded crusader counterpart.

'Spider-Man!'

I skipped to a stop and looked up. Hanging from a second floor window was half a girl. She wasn't literally half a girl, it was just I could only actually see one half of her, the top half. The other half was inside her flat. She was leaning out of the window, balancing, and carefully vomiting down the side of the building and onto the window of the poor sap who happened to have been roomed beneath her.

'Spider-Man, I'm being sick'.

With the mask on, and the blood pumping through my veins rather than crawling through them as usual I felt alive and dangerous, a completely different person from the meek personality who would sit in his room waiting and listening out for the kitchen to clear of flatmates so he could go in and make himself beans on toast for dinner.

'Do you need assistance ma'am?' Spider-Man shouted up to her.

Where the fuck did that come from? I thought

'I've been sick Spider-Man. Help me!'

'I can see that' Spider-Man said.

'Help me' she repeated.

By this point I was completely lost in the role-play. I didn't know what Spider-Man would say next. I wasn't in charge.

'I'm coming up' Spider-Man said.

For some reason her boyfriend chose this moment to appear behind her, almost blocking the light with his bulk. His neck was as wide as his head and his shoulders were as wide as the window. He wore a vest to perfectly demonstrate these proportions.

'Piss off mate' he shouted down at me, and pulled his dribbling girlfriend in, away from the window. She just had time to wave to Spider-Man as she was dragged off. With a crashing defeat I reverted back to being Michael, a mild mannered first year law student who thought he would never find love and would break gender conventions by becoming a crazy old cat man. With that conclusion secure in my mind I walked back to my flat and the admiration of my flatmates.

Two nights later I was back in the same one-piece costume, feeling rather self-conscious about how it made my genitals look and walking to the bar with two vampires, a sexy witch and a sexy cat. We had been 'pre-drinking' since *Deal Or No Deal* and combined with the limited vision my stocking-like mask afforded me I wasn't feeling too rosy. I could feel my hot vodka breath bouncing around within the confines of the mask. I worried it was having the same effect on me as sticking a hose in the exhaust pipe of a car and sucking that.

'Here you go Mike, get this down you'.

A foggy looking bottle of something alcoholic was passed in front of me. I succeeded in getting it down me, completely. I went to swig from the bottle and forgot the mask covered my mouth. The liquid met with cloth and the effect was similar to what I imagine being smothered to feel like. I spat and spluttered drink from my mouth and nose as I ripped off the mask and gasped at the night air.

'Wahey!' one of them screamed, 'looks like someone can't handle their booze'.

They were all more than aware by then how true the statement was yet this was different. I had developed a reputation for bringing up the holy trinity of dinner, drinks and stomach lining after a night out however I wouldn't class choking in a mask as being in the same category. I am sure in some fields of S&M there are people who would get off on such activities, like the men who hang-wank themselves to death. I feel I should rather fervently state now, up to this point in my life I have not experimented with hang-wanking in any way, shape or form.

By the time we got to the bar I was fed up with the two vampires, the sexy witch and the sexy cat and decided to just get absolutely ruined and make a scene of myself. It turned out to be a lot easier than I had anticipated. The mask seemed to help. It not only gave me the kind of anonymity one always desires when drunk, it also seemed to exacerbate the effects of alcohol, creating a strange kind of claustrophobia so I consistently felt both sick and dizzy. I was suddenly approached by two vampires who seemed to recognise me.

'It's Michael right?' said the white vampire.

I took the mask off to get a better look at him.

'Yeah?' I asked.

'I'm Harry. You know, from your class. This is Jay' he said, pointing to the black vampire.

'Nice to meet ya' I managed, the Essex drawl I hid so well when sober sneaking into my pronunciation.

'Yeah, right. Who are you here with?' asked Jay.

'Two vampires, a sexy witch and a sexy cat'.

'Right, cool. Where did you get the costume from?' asked Harry.

'Woolworths' I replied too honestly.

'What size is it?'

'Eight to ten years'.

They both found this hilarious for some reason. I felt I had found my audience and had obviously been too quick to assume everyone else in my class was boring.

'Look at the wrists' I said. 'These gloves are supposed to get over my hands but they just sort of wobble halfway up my forearms'.

'Why the hell are you wearing that?'

'I didn't fancy being a sexy cat' I replied, hilarious as ever.

'Come on' said my new mate Harry, 'let's get you a drink'.

As it turned out I had been spotted and judged by the other people in my law lectures in the same way I had made assumptions about them. While I had taken those first weeks to either gaze out of the window, or write a series of lyrics and short stories in my carefully selected notepads they had been trying to work me out. They could tell what I was writing were not notes based on what the lecturer had been saying but they couldn't pin me down beyond that. Dressing up as Spider-Man had been the decisive move.

From that night on Harry and I were firm friends. You shouldn't worry this is the conclusion of the story, I'm just taking a moment to explain how we met. The interesting bit is still to come. It's the bit Harry likes to tell as well, because it was embarrassing for us both.

A black vampire, a white vampire and Spider-Man walk into a bar. It sounds like a good setup for a joke.

The only joke was the amount of Tequila they made me drink. It gave me the idea I was a terrific dancer, something almost anyone including myself could tell you is definitely not the case. I can barely walk down a set of stairs without fucking it up, let alone move like Jagger. I truly went wild that night. With my mask on I was sure everyone would just approve of me, and want to dance with Spider-Man. I thought they would gather around me for group photos and then we could all dance like robots from 1984 together. It turned out while they found it mildly amusing, there is something very disconcerting and sinister about someone dancing too close to you wearing what would best be described as a child's gymnastics costume.

Before long I found the only person who would dance with me was the girl painted up as the Incredible Hulk. By day she went by the name Kerry.

Looking back on that evening with the wonderful power of hindsight it does seem a little bit weird for a number of reasons. The first is, why would any level-headed young lady dress up as the Hulk, a character who is neither a sexy witch nor a slutty cat? The second is why would said girl choose to dance with a boy squeezed into a children's Halloween costume? I assume you have come to the same conclusion I have since, she must be in some way unstable. What an onlooker like Harry saw, was Spider-Man and the Incredible Hulk entering into some kind of primal dance, circling one another, arms raised like crab's claws, legs stretched wide like rugby aces. Apparently we danced in that fashion for about half an hour before it all got a bit too much for Spider-Man. I pulled my mask off, smiling at the girl with green face paint sweating down onto her ripped white t-shirt.

'Wow' she said, 'you look like Pete Doherty'.

I remember that line very well because it's a very backhanded compliment and won me over completely.

'Do you want a drink?' I asked.

'Yeah, vodka and lemonade please'.

I did as I was told. An hour later the lights came on and we shielded our eyes as we realised the night was over and we were still in each other's company. I couldn't exactly call it being *with* her because nothing had been contracted and in my naïve way I thought that was the way these things had to be done. She invited me back to hers regardless.

As it turned out Harry had recently had some kind of dalliance with Kerry's flatmate Lori and had decided he wanted to walk back with us and surprise her by turning up on her doorstep. To me and my drink-addled brain this seemed like the sweetest and most noble idea I had ever heard. By this stage of the evening I had undone the Velcro back of my costume and stripped the top half from my unimpressive torso. This left me dressed in what were essentially cycling shorts.

When we got back to the flat I was led into Kerry's room so she could de-Hulk herself. She offered me a hoodie because I was sat on her bed shivering in half a costume. I put it on but left it undone. Harry disappeared off to knock on Lori's door. I tried to take in everything that was going on through the drunken mesh settling on my brain. It looked to me as though she had been living in that room for years rather than the month or so we had been on campus. There were stacks of magazines on music, nursing (her chosen area of study) and fashion. There were DVDs collected along the full length of the shelves. There were layers of posters on the walls. Even the curtains looked different to the ones supplied as standard. It looked more like a bedroom than a dorm room. While I had been passing judgement over her room Kerry had been using up a whole pack of face wipes getting the green paint off her skin. It was the first time I had fully seen her face properly and despite the slightly ill hue it maintained it wasn't an unpretty face to look upon.

At that stage in my life I had kissed a total of five girls, and was very much of the belief that somewhere out there was that special someone who would complete my life in every single way possible. I thought that person was the other half of me somehow, we would go together and just be a complete little jigsaw. I would never want for anything else and our love alone would finance the rest of our lives.

In that moment I realised Kerry wasn't the yin to my yang but in my drunken way it didn't seem to matter. I wanted to feel wanted, and the way she looked at me was what I would now call greed or lust, but at the time I just took for being appreciation of my form. I was a double underlined <u>virgin</u> at that point. That's also an important item to note as it makes the way I went about things in general seem a lot more reasonable.

The insane panic you somehow owe everyone you ever have sex with something, as though it means you are bound together in the way when dogs fuck the male will turn and lock in his partner to ensure no other male can ruin the good times by asserting their dominance. That is what I thought of sex. As though it were this terrifying, all encompassing thing it felt like everyone else was enjoying and meanwhile I was terrified of. It's the stuff of *17* or *Sugar* magazine and isn't something teenage boys feel willing to discuss. It felt as though everyone else was indulging in it though.

As I tried to establish exactly what I was going to do and how I was going to explain how I felt about the situation, and how my own insecurities might stop me from being at the top of my game. How I wasn't sure about all this and did she believe in soul mates and if she did would it not be better to just wait for them. As I was weighing up all of these heavy scales, Kerry walked over, pushed me down on the bed and somewhat sexily, somewhat drunkenly, fell on top of me.

As I left her bedroom at around four o'clock in the morning I nearly tripped over Harry who was curled up in a ball outside the door to Lori's room.

'I don't think she's coming home mate' I said to him.

'Oh? What's the time then?' he asked, unravelling sleepily.

'It's coming up to four. Do you want to walk back with me?'

'Yeah, I suppose I had better. This bitch doesn't know what she's missing' he said as though it would hurt the empty room's feelings.

We made our way down the stairs and I pulled the hood up on the jumper Kerry had let me borrow. I lit up a cigarette.

'Do you live in St Christopher's?' I asked.

'Nah, I'm over in St Johns'.

'Do you want me to walk you back?'

'Nah, I'm alright' he said, putting his hand straight up in the air and walking in the wrong direction.

'Harry, this way' I said and started towards the general area I knew his flat was in.

That night secured our friendship. From then on we were near enough inseparable. At one point I moved into Harry's flat, living underneath the stairs. It was during my time there Sophie moved in.

Harry fell for her completely. They fell for each other in fact. While I was putting my newly unwrapped tackle to the test, Harry was spending his time being well and truly in love, wearing a dressing gown around the flat and generally just growing up. By the time I moved into their flat legitimately they were like my parents. Harry would make sure I got up and went to lectures, regardless of how little sleep I had got, and Sophie would ensure I ate, regardless of how hungover I was. The stories they continue to tell of me to this day are those of a lost boy, a hedonist who nosedived for the thrill of it, and managed to make it out of the spin intact. When Harry first told me he had asked Sophie to marry him I tried everything within my power to convince him he was making a massive mistake. I told him nobody finds the one person they want to be with forever when they are nineteen. I felt he had plenty to give, and shouldn't give up so soon. Fortunately he didn't listen to a word of it and by the time he got around to asking me to be his best man I was over the moon about it all. The thing they made me realise, as a couple, is although it might not be perfect, it was enough. Humans aren't perfect. I've learnt that. As a perfect example, I'm far from it. The idea of some perfect love is completely impossible. You just have those who can make it work, and those who can't and they found one who could a lot sooner than I did.

****

I dropped the sheet of paper back to the table. I hadn't needed it. It had just become a prop to my act of being the best man. I spent the speech with it pincered between the thumb and forefinger of my left hand while the index finger of my right ran along the smooth edges.

Later Harry would express some concern over the fact the much caressed and folded copy of the speech I gave them to put in their wedding book was not the speech I had delivered. I had to tell him I had just let the words pour out of me. What I felt and what I wanted to say were not the things I had written, so with a bottle of wine inside me I spoke from the heart, and that could never be contained.

Home

RYAN
November 2006

'How long are you back for then?' Noah asked me over the sound of people who could never get enough of a 'double up for an extra £1' promotion in a pub.

'Just this weekend'.

'Oh right. What are you studying again?'

'Business marketing', I replied with a near sigh. 'It's alright. I don't even remember sometimes'. It sounded a lot funnier in my head. It didn't bother me all that much. Nobody remembered. I wouldn't have expected Noah to know. He wasn't my parents and he wasn't my girlfriend, because I didn't have one. He certainly isn't me so why should I expect him to remember such a trivial detail. I sure as hell couldn't remember what he was studying.

'What are you studying?' I asked to show I could be just as nonchalant about his future as he seemed to be being about my own.

'I'm not. I'm working'.

'Oh right' I said.

It is always a struggle when conversations reach a natural dead end and yet both parties are stood dumbly staring into each other's faces. I started off on the whole university thing to avoid getting a job, putting in the hard work and climbing the corporate ladder. I would much rather spend three years getting pissed and then be catapulted in above all the mess.

'Yeah, it's going well' he said without me asking.

'Good'.

Noah looked over my shoulder, trying to think outside the pair of us, and then ushered to someone with a wave.

'Ryan, this is my girlfriend Claire'.

A completely bland and predictably mousy type girl approached us. I could not possibly draw any of her features out for description, she was just a thing.

'This is Ryan, babe' he said to her.

'Nice to meet you Ryan' she said, avoiding eye contact and lying simultaneously. She raised her hand feebly and when I met it with my own her touch was cold and frail.

'Nice to meet you too' I replied smiling, despite the fact it wasn't and I probably would never see her again, or remember if I were to meet her again.

The odds were I wouldn't have to meet her again because Noah's relationships worked on a highly predictable cycle. This had been the case since we were at school together, and actually had something in common and considered ourselves friends. The first couple of months of any of his relationships are smooth sailing, but then they work out how boring he is and leave him. Each time this causes Noah to fall apart and collapse on the kitchen floor singing along to Donna Summer. It's as certain as the changing of the seasons.

Being at home was entirely predictable and therefore entirely boring. I wondered if it would be possible for me to leave, get on a train and be back at university sooner than the drive back with my old man on the Sunday evening would allow. Unfortunately I concluded it wasn't. It wouldn't have been possible to make the connections. At the end of the day I would rather use my small allowance to get pissed, than to get the train.

I missed Caera and Bark, the people I had been with for just three months but already felt completely understood by. It had been an intense time in all of our lives, spending literally every day from fresher's week onward in one another's company. It was like having that first proper girlfriend, the one you end up completely abandoning your friends for. You declare the people who had stuck by you to be completely useless and just fall for one person with everything you've got. Of course in time you realise how flawed that one person is, and how wrong you were to be together in the first place, and you realise you have to escape.

The key thing to remember is I was still very much in the 'honeymoon phase' with my new uni friends. I doted on them, and I continue to maintain contact and relationships with them to this day, when there are thousands of miles stood between us and our very different lives. They are still very precious to me and I hope they can hold that thought, and memories of me, and be aware of it.

'Will you excuse me one minute, I've just seen someone' I said. I walked away from Noah and Claire who were mid-flow about something I didn't understand. I headed towards the bar, sweeping through groups of friends huddled around tables without enough chairs, talking over each other. Everyone looked very different to how I felt. It was all very showy and dressed up and I was just in a Belle & Sebastian t-shirt and skinny jeans.

I eventually shouldered through enough people and made it to the bar, just about managing to clinch a few fingers onto the marble surface to stake my territory, to show my place in the world.

It seemed the staff had no regard or concern for the desperate need for alcohol possessing my mouth and throat. I needed to be away from people like Noah and

Claire for a while and if that meant getting dangerously drunk then so be it. Sometimes the best of things take place when you really have very little control.

The girl directly in front of me finished paying for her drinks and turned around with three chunky glasses of vibrant cocktails balanced between her trembling fingers. I stood aside the best I could in the crowd to allow her to pass and then sealed the space at the bar with my body.

Beside me stood a man in his late thirties desperately trying to be served. His hair was scraped back from his face and heavily coated with the cheap, wet-look gel everyone dragged through their follicles in the 90's. He was wearing an ill-fitting suit jacket with the sleeves rolled up his hairy forearms, and there was a twenty-pound note pincered between his bronzed, sweating fingers. In profile he had the look of the missing link, the charming mix of ape and man Charlton Heston had spent so much time evading.

Each time a barman passed by he would wave his money at them as though he was doing them a massive favour directly with his mighty order.

I've spent time working in bars and pubs and can tell you it doesn't matter at all if you are waving a note at a barman. There is already an established order to proceedings. A barman will always aim to serve the pretty girls first, often free-pouring spirits with a cheeky wink. Then they will serve their friends. It is only after this anyone else will get a look in. My tip would therefore be to put away your cut with pharmaceuticals cocaine-tinged note back in your faux leather wallet and wait patiently like everyone else you self righteous, arrogant prick.

I smugly got my own order in before Mr Sweaty-Sweepback, and sauntered off to try and find someone I could make conversation with. There were a large group of my friends from college gathered around in a circle not far off from the bar. I stood on the limits, the circumference, waiting for an in, or something I could laugh at and feel associated. Nobody addressed my approach directly. After two minutes I decided to go outside for a cigarette.

At this time in my life I was using smoking to counter a number of things in my life; boredom, what I considered to be stress, hunger, society. It did a fantastic job. Since then I have found ways to cope with most of the above and smoking has fallen by the wayside like so many other vices and people I had previously held so tightly.

I made for the door and was stopped in my tracks by a girl in a bar uniform who was approximately two thirds my height.

'Are you going outside?' she asked.

'Me?'

'Yeah. Are you going outside?'

I noticed she was holding a stack of dirty plastic pint glasses across her chest.

'Yeah, I am. Why? Do you want a cigarette?' I asked, instantly reaching into my back pocket for my pack and offering them up to her.

'No. Smoking is disgusting. It's just, you can't take your drink out there'.

'Why?'

'We aren't allowed glass out the front of the building'.

'Why not?'

'Because every Saturday night there is a fight, loads of them get smashed. We can't afford to keep buying new ones, and I don't want to have to clear up broken glass'.

'Oh' I said.

I took a single cup from her and converted my rum and coke into it. By the time I got outside what she had said was starting to really bother me. They had so many fights in the pub they'd been forced to take preventative measures to limit the damage. At uni I had seen five hundred pissed up students leave a venue without so much as a punch being thrown.

In fact I struggle to think of any fights I ever saw on campus. There was just no need for it the majority of the time. I'm sure there must have been some, because some people on campus deserved to get a kicking once in a while but it wasn't the same as brawling violence. It was a more gentlemanly pursuit. It had decorum. It was more like rounds of fisticuffs. The thought of the boys of Essex indulging in bouts of street fighting really put me off the thought of spending the night out. There was always the danger I would be the one the switchblade got pulled on. The one who ended up getting done in for no reason.

I didn't want to be a Tybalt.

As I finished the cigarette my group of friends emerged from the pub and stopped in silence when they spotted me.

'Oh, there you are Ryan. Come on. We are going to The Jack'.

If you aren't a local then you won't know The Jack was our local nightspot. It was the only place in our tiny town that had a license to stay open until two in the morning. The music was generally better than the jukebox trash blasted out of the pubs along the high street. The floors were sticky, which aided in the pursuit of the fairer sex, because they simply couldn't escape.

I stood up and my usual row of insecurities started being shot down like tin cans on a wall. I wondered if my friends would have come to find me if I hadn't been sat outside, perched between them and The Jack. I wondered if they would have abandoned me inside the pub, or if they would have sent a search party back inside to try and collect me before they continued on. I hoped it was the latter.

I stubbed my cigarette out under the sole of my shoe and stood to walk with them down the street.

'Alright Ry, where've you been?' asked Adam, another friend who had fallen from my radar in recent months.

'Uni and that' I replied.

'Oh yeah, what are you studying?'

Two hours later I was trying to compose myself in the black-walled toilet cubicle of The Jack. All I could hear was the bass of the sound system and all I could feel was the knot of what had formerly been my dinner pogoing between my stomach and oesophagus. My head was thumping to the beat of the music and I needed a minute to just reassure myself, to breath and to calm down. I took my still-full pint from the window ledge over the toilet bowl, and bursting out from behind the cubicle door poured it down the sink and ran the dripping tap above. I washed the plastic pint glass out and then filled it with water. I drank about two pints, throwing a minimal amount down the front of my t-shirt.

As I stood mopping my eyes and mouth with the back of my hand, I heard someone calling my name. I span a full circle but couldn't find the source. I thought it had just been inside my head, that somehow vomiting so violently had affected my hearing. I went back to drying my eyes and it happened again. This time I turned and just caught sight of the side of a face poking slyly out from behind the other cubicle door.

It was Wayne. A guy I had worked with in the kitchen of a restaurant the previous Summer, before I had gone away to uni. It had been a time in my life when I was supposed to be saving up money for books and supplies but instead was just pissing the pathetic wages I got up the wall after hours. If it taught me anything it was that nobody is as funny when they are drunk as they think they are. We all turn into twats when we've had too much.

Wayne looked out at me with big wide eyes and pinprick pupils, like a wolf. There was something desperate and savage in it. I knew that look like a reflection.

'Can you watch the door for me?'

I knew straight away what was going on. I made a move towards the doorway to the bathroom, feeling a lot more sober than I had an instant before. Over the sound of my own shifting breaths I could hear Wayne snorting heavily from behind the closed door. There was a clatter and he emitted a deep sigh.

My eyes kept flocking from his cubicle to the long expanse of corridor that separated the toilets from the mass of the club. Somehow I didn't see the two bouncers in their bright yellow t-shirts until they were virtually on top of me.

I started coughing, partly out of fear, partly out of surprise but mostly because I knew it would act as a good warning to Wayne who was loudly fiddling about with something.

The bouncers rushed into the toilet, scanning the room for wanton drug users they could give a harsh beating to in the darkened hallway before they got them to the exit where CCTV disrupted their fun.

One of them slammed the door to Wayne's cubicle open. He had heeded my warning and put his works away, even having time to produce his cock from his trousers and feign genuine use of the toilet.

'Sorry guys, did you want to watch?' he asked. They just glared at him like Orcs on the prowl before moving on like they hadn't eaten anything but maggoty bread for three stinking days.

'Thanks mate' Wayne said, once they had cleared off. 'Did you want a bump?'

I can't remember if I nodded but I found myself back in the cubicle with a bag of white powder and Wayne's snooker club membership card. Fearing I could be set upon at any moment by the gruesome bouncers I dabbed my finger into the bag and wiped the residue on my upper gums. It felt cool in every sense of the word. I had seen people test drugs in films that way. It had the aftertaste however of tablets. I concluded it was probably just the result of whatever it had been cut with. As I emerged from the toilet Wayne grinned at me.

'Did you get enough?'

'Yeah, it was fine' I said, rubbing my tongue over the raised tingle above my teeth.

'There's plenty more where that came from'.

'Oh right, cool'.

'-if you hang out with me tonight'. It was a strange offer. I thought about the alternatives, quickly dismissed them all and was left feeling somewhat intrigued.

'Why? What's the matter?'

'I need one night to get categorically destroyed. Wayne has been a naughty boy' he replied, with a glint in his brown eye. His top lip twitched to meet it. 'Let's just say I have got myself into a bit of bother over a woman, or more specifically two women, and I have to face the music tomorrow. I would just like to get lost in tonight. I need a wingman. How do you feel about that?'

'I'm game' I quickly replied.

'That's good. Let's get a Sambuca'.

Usually I am not a fan of the dreaded shot. I would go so far as to say if Sambuca were a person, it would cross over the road to avoid talking to me. That is how badly we got on. If Sambuca was someone I knew it would definitely not remember what I was studying at university, that much is certain.

I couldn't resist Wayne's charms though, and I say that in a completely straight way, if that is possible. He was in need of a friend and I felt I was too, so I fell into line behind him as we headed back out into the mayhem and over to the bar which had a space which seemed to be set aside just for us to slide into.

'What are you drinking?' he asked me.

I knew I couldn't have another pint.

'Why?'

'Well I'll drink whatever it is you're drinking, I'll match you'.

'Rum and coke please' I said, feeling slightly like a spoilt rent boy.

'Alright mate' Wayne said to the barman, 'two rum and cokes and two Sambucas please'. After placing the order Wayne turned back to me. 'How is uni going?'

'Yeah, it's not bad thanks'. I waited for the inevitable.

'What is it you are studying again?'

I went to speak.

'-Business Marketing right?' he said.

'Yeah, that's right'.

'Sorry, I interrupted. What were you going to say?'

'Nothing' I replied, and collected my fresh rum and coke from the counter.

As it turned out the cocaine I had been given was pretty good. I noted as we made our way over to the dance floor I was under the grand illusion I could dance. This was a thought process I reserved for when I was on drugs. Sober Ryan would never take to the dance floor, unless it was to cross it, at speed, on the way to the bar.

Club Foot by Kasabian started playing and I span around on my pointed toes, circling one hand up above my head and then down in big windmills like Pete Townsend. I am glad there is no CCTV on the inside of The Jack because I would hate to see what I looked like. All I genuinely believed in the moment was that I was the king of rock 'n' roll and the duke of fuck.

'I'm going to the toilet, are you coming?' Wayne asked, as the song disappeared off and was cross-faded into something else. It was the only time in my life I had heard those words from a man and not worried I was about to be bummed to death with a urinal cake in my mouth.

I followed Wayne loyally back down the passageway and stood at the entrance to the toilet, nodding to guys as they went in and out as though I were the guardian of the urinals.

Wayne emerged looking particularly ragged. The patches of his face I could see through the week's worth of stubble were pale and clammy looking. His eyes were running wild.

'You alright?' I asked.

'Yeah, you're up. I left it all on the top of the cistern. Fill your boots'.

With my nose abuzz with white excitement we headed off to one of the seated booths to host a lively chat about exactly why we thought the other was just about the best guy in the world.

'The thing is man' I said, sniffing automatically, 'you don't care what people think. You're just Wayne, take it or leave it and-'.

'Yeah, but I'm not man, I-'.

'Woah. Woah. Let me finish. I mean you are just-'.

'Let's have a cigarette'.

'Yeah, cool!'

It continued from exactly where we had left off as soon as we got outside. I leant back against the cool brickwork and let Wayne light the cigarette dangling from my lips.

'You know who you are, and you know where you're going, and that's so cool. I admire you. I love you man'.

We finished smoking while nervously jabbering to one another, patting each other on the back and making promises of drug deals, business ventures and nights out which would probably never come to fruition.

We were sat back in the same booth moments later when Wayne alerted me to someone staring at me across the room.

'That girl keeps staring at you'.

At first I thought it was just his paranoia, but when I looked over to where his eyes were indicating, there was indeed a girl staring at us. She wasn't just a girl though, she was a girl I had once dated and then spectacularly dumped for another girl who I had then dumped for my friends and so on.

She wasn't looking at me through torn up eyes like I would have imagined. I like to imagine all the girls I have ever been in contact with stood on a widow's peak, dressed in black, looking out at the tumultuous sea, and awaiting my safe return.

'Go over and speak to her' Wayne said. 'She obviously digs you'.

She was sat with a group of her friends who I had never met, because in the couple of months we had been *together* I had refused to spend time with her friends, because I'm the tragic bastard type.

'Nat' I said, taking a seat too close to her without permission. I couldn't work out how I had gone from being sat beside Wayne to getting up, walking across the expanse between us, and sitting beside her but there I was.

'Ryan, you look rough. Are you okay?'

'Yeah, I'm fine. I was just wondering if maybe I could buy you a drink' I said, suddenly very self-aware.

'Not really. I'm with my friends' she replied, gesturing behind her.

'I can see that, I just thought I would offer'.

I stood up and was just about to return to Wayne when I realised he was already beside me. The change in his position threw me more than my own had. It was as though he had jumped forward in time. For some reason this had the effect I had desired upon Natalie and she stood to join us.

'I guess one drink would be okay' she said, and took my hand. Wayne quickly spotted the action and raised his eyebrows at me knowingly.

'This is Wayne' I eventually managed to say, and they hugged hello as she still held onto me. We headed off to the bar as the last of *Honest Mistake* played out.

'What did I fucking tell you' said Wayne, leaning into my ear so Natalie couldn't make out the conversation on my other side. I nudged him into silence momentarily.

'What are you drinking?' I asked Natalie.

'Why?'

'Because we will have three of those' I replied, employing the same technique Wayne had in order to assimilate with the target.

'Vodka and coke'.

'Lovely' I said.

'What can I get you?' mouthed the barman over the sound of The Courteeners.

'Three vodka cokes, and three Sambucas' I shouted back.

'Not for me' said Nat, 'I hate it, don't you remember?'

She had caught me out. There had been a few girls since her and sometimes it was hard to keep track on the drinking habits of them all. Once she had mentioned it the memory came flying back. How on our first date we had talked about drinking etiquette, and the art of the binge our generation seemed so fond of, and she had explicitly said she'd had too many bad experiences on it and the smell alone was enough to set her off. I had agreed. At the time I thought it was one of the many things we had in common and could share forever.

'Make that three Jägers' I said to the barman eventually.

Nat stared straight into my eyes as she knocked back the test tube Jägermeister is always served in for some reason. She then up-ended the vodka and coke, draining the cup, and holding the ice back with pursed lips and teeth.

'Do you want a cigarette?' she asked, carefully blotting her lips with the back of her hand.

'When did you start smoking?' I replied, genuinely shocked. She had always been so vehemently antismoking while we had been together. Although she was one of the few girls who didn't try to convince me to quit, because that signalled an attempt to change me, and she would have been out of the door a lot sooner.

'I started smoking' she said, poking me in the chest and stepping back drunkenly with the force she had exerted, 'when you broke up with me because I missed the smell'.

'You hated the smell!' I replied, holding her upright by the shoulder.

'I guess I didn't'.

She led me back outside. Wayne followed, keeping his distance, and eyeing up the girls and the bouncers in equal measures.

When we got outside the fresh air and the alcohol hit Natalie and she fell against me, her cigarette hand suspended just before her face as she slid down my shirt. In the light of the evening she looked better than I could ever remember. I couldn't work out exactly what I had been thinking when I had decided we weren't right together, and that I wanted to pursue someone else. I couldn't find anything. I had fallen completely all over again. I wanted to look after her, and be there for her, and never leave her or make her angry again.

'Natalie, are you drunk?'

'What's in it for you?'

'Do you need to go home?' I asked.

'*Do you need to go home?*' she repeated, mocking me. She looked up at me, right into my eyes and I knew we were about to kiss and my brain jumped to novocaine action and performed a quick bit of arithmetic:

Ryan + drunken ex + kissing = good times

In my drink and drug-addled mind it seemed like the most logical conclusion. I shut my eyes and carefully pushed my head out onto the chopping block. Our lips met and buzzed together and then we kissed fully. I couldn't help but hold back, worried about where her reckless hand and attached cigarette had got to. As we parted she lifted her hand to her mouth, took one final drag, and then stamped it under her boot. She blew the smoke up into the night air, and kissed me again, hard.

'Take me home' she said.

'Yours or mine?' I replied, smooth as fuck.

'Yours'.

I quickly said goodbye to Wayne who had apparently moved on. The last image I have of him that evening was him laughing, one hand snaked around an attractive blonde in a low cut top.

'See you later' he yelled as I took Natalie's hand and we headed for the taxi rank.

Because The Jack hadn't yet decided to kick the punters to the curb we had our choice of cabs. Our choice of Bernard or Gary or Steve. Our choice of a saloon, a black cab, a six seater.

'Alright mate' I called into the open window of the black cab, 'can we jump in?'

'Just get in the front one mate' he bellowed back, assuming I was drunk and barely coherent when in fact the fresh air had cleared my head. We made our way to the front of the line, hand in hand.

I held the door for her and then slid in myself.

'South View please mate' I said to the cabbie, instantly aware the only time I ever used the word *mate* was when I spoke to someone providing me with a service. It always led me to immediately worry I was terribly middle class for changing my vernacular and then even worse for spotting myself doing it. We got halfway back to my house before Natalie was able to get her head into gear.

'Oh shit, I have work tomorrow' she said.

'That's alright. You can crash at mine, and I'll give you a lift home in the morning'. She smiled guiltily.

'I have work at seven tomorrow'.

'That's alright. We can hang out, I'll take you for lunch somewhere, and then-'. In my head I had been trying to work out if I could borrow some money from my parents in order to be able to take her out for lunch. In a way it was lucky she interrupted me.

'I have work at seven in the morning'.

My mind performed another piece of arithmetic.

'That's in five and a half hours' I spluttered.

'Yeah, that's why I wasn't supposed to get drunk' she replied, biting her lip as though she had only just remembered.

'This is okay. We can do that. We'll just get back to mine, and go to bed. You really only need four hours sleep to process, and then I'll take you home in the morning' I said, knowing I wasn't planning on sleeping (as long as the cocaine hadn't completely ceased the opportunity of an erection).

Natalie finally conceded and in silence we pulled up outside my house. I paid and then ran around to open her door for her, pulling out all the stops, pretending I was a gentleman. I then used my usual line.

'We will have to be quiet, my flatmates are asleep'.

'Ryan' she said, 'I've been round before, I know you live with your parents'. It caught me entirely off guard. I used it as a simple reflex action, like catching something thrown at your face.

'Yeah, I know. I was making a joke'.

Moments later we were upstairs, and in our underwear and she was planting a series of kisses from my neck, down to the elasticated top of my boxer shorts.

She then hooked her thumbs in and slowly brought them down to below my knees. I heard the slap of my erection on my belly and breathed an audible sigh of relief that the drugs hadn't ruined my chances of getting laid before my personality could.

She began by kissing the tip, and then she looked up at me through the darkness before taking me entirely in her mouth. There was a sense of familiarity to it all. I remembered it had in fact been Natalie's forte. I watched the light pollution of the street outside the mostly closed curtains as her head intermittently bobbed, her hair sweeping and brushing against my naked belly and thighs.

In the list of pros and cons I had mentally drawn up when trying to decide if I was going to dismiss our relationship, this ability had been a most definite pro. I sunk my head back into the pillow and dreamt of England. This essentially meant trying to enjoy and ultimately get lost in the moment, embracing how good it felt while simultaneously worrying about how long a blowjob could go on for, and whether a girl expected to make you ejaculate by doing so. Is it considered bad form not to reach orgasm at her fair mouth?

I wondered if I should try to think of something else, something off-putting in order to hold myself back. Would there be sex?

I concluded there most definitely would be. It would be best to try and think of something dark and horrible in order to hold back from that glorious precipice. The problem I had was laying in the dark with the clock slowly approaching two I couldn't think of anything. I was drawing a spectacular blank. My mind was buzzing completely but it was with the static lines of cocaine abuse, no longer with logic or decipherable thought, and so it was I came to the conclusion I was about to release.

'Oh, I'm going to come' I said, pulling myself out from the depths of the pillow I was arching back into. I was hit with the sudden rushing of my soul to my penis, as though it were being drawn like poison from a wound. My entire body seized up, as though I were crumbling up under an incredible heat. I felt muscles I didn't know I had contract. I was lost and it felt pure and good, and all was right in the world for that split second. I was on cloud nine. I was on a high drugs could not meet. I was playing Woodstock.

Natalie chose this moment to remove my penis from her mouth, presumably to protect herself from an onslaught of semen, and pushed it away from her. She chose to push it away from where she was laying, curled between my buckling legs, with her own feet pushed against the metal frame of the end of my bedstead. She pointed my erupting penis away from herself and up towards my stomach right on queue.

In a moment of pure joy I came, and the ejaculate shot up at me like Barnes-Wallis's bouncing bomb. With my cranked up reflexes I managed to turn my head just in time, so the spunk skimmed my cheek, and then flipped up, splattering on my hair like a pearly water balloon.

I screamed.

I'm not proud to admit it, but I screamed.

'Ahhh, there's spunk in my hair!'

From between my knees I heard a giggle. I realised I had my eyes closed tight, and my face scrunched together as though it were constricted. My breathing was fast, irregular and rattling. I hadn't yet released my body from the lock of orgasm.

'This isn't funny' I said, going limp, and grabbing down the side of my bed for a discarded t-shirt. I managed to get most of the offending goods out of my hair, and off of my face but I couldn't escape the feeling I would wake up like Ken Dodd.

By the time Natalie stopped laughing I had recovered and was ready to go again. It was the last time I got to be with her.

Amsterdam

MICHAEL
February 2006

It was the way she watched the clock as the bed made each complete turn around the room that really freaked me out. She had the bored expression of a woman waiting for a bus, avoiding eye contact and staring off into an unfathomable distance thinking of a life been and gone. For me the situation was far from humdrum.

Her co-star wasn't particularly tactful either, going at the metaphorical canvas with a stabbing motion straight out of a Hitchcock film. He was not painting a pretty picture.

Inside the booth we held our collective breath. There was me, and my friend Zach, the intrepid explorers. Then there was his flatmate Zara who was in my law class and of the fiery redhead category. There was also her friend Catherine, who was the first real lesbian I ever met, and then there was Dalpat (or Dal as everyone called him) who was a complete anomaly and dark horse to me during the trip but who soon become a good friend. We all watched as beyond a single sheet of glass, a man and a woman lay completely naked on a revolving bed, having sex, for our supposed amusement. It clearly was not for theirs.

The booths were arranged in a circle, all facing in on the bedroom, and all with a peep window like ours. The difference was the faces in those other windows were far more eager, a fact proven by the toilet roll holder installed in each of the cells.

Feeling slightly sick, either from watching a live sex act or because of the motion sickness watching a bed revolve can cause, I decided to look up, beyond the fucking couple and into the other windows. It freaked me out. I couldn't believe how ordinary they looked. It could have been the weed changing my perception.

A man occupied every other booth. Some looked around our age, but some looked a lot older, as though they could have families of their own. They looked like they could have been fathers, or doctors, or lawyers, or somehow a combination of all three. Here they all were, watching a slim blonde girl count down the last few seconds until the end of her shift of being fucked.

Imagine going home after that:

'Evening honey, how was your day?'

'Oh, not too bad, I'm *fucking* knackered though'.

It hadn't been as much fun as I had assumed when the idea was originally suggested. It was however remarkably inexpensive considering the content, just two Euro coins jammed into the slot (not that one) on the inside of the booth. The payment allowed the lights to dim in our cage and we could see through the looking glass, and into the bedroom. I'm not going to get all *Wish You Were Here* about it but if you're looking for a cheap day out for the family....

'I'm going to wait outside' Zara eventually said.

There was a moment of sweet cool air as the door at the back of the unit was opened and she slipped out. I had not realised until that point just how stuffy it had become with the five of us rammed in a room not much larger than a phone box.

I couldn't look away from the couple. There was something hypnotic about the motion, like sitting and watching a Newton's Cradle. At the same time as my enjoyment there was also a schoolboy-like guilt, as though my own mother was about to rip the door open, pull me out by my ear and make me wash my eyes out for seeing such disgusting filth. As it happens she was over three hundred miles away in Essex, but a little thing like that won't stop a Jewish mother.

With a grinding sound the light suddenly cut out. In the darkness we heard our two Euro pieces drop into the abyss. We were plunged back into an awkward blackness, worried about making physical contact with each other but desperate to reach out for the exit. Suddenly one of the others made contact with the door, light poured in and we all fell out laughing into the main body of the porn shop which housed the peep show.

As my eyes adjusted to the light I could see Zara impatiently waiting just outside the door, her green eyes attempting to usher us along a little quicker.

'Where are we going now then?' asked Zach, swaggering his way towards the exit.

'Wait, I'm not done in here' said Catherine, before turning to me. 'Come on Michael, show me the porn you like'.

This blew my mind. It was not the kind of sentence I had heard from a young lady's mouth before. I imagined them all to be sat around fanning themselves at the mere mention of a torso, yet here was this girl openly inviting me to look through stacks of porn with her. I stood dumbstruck as she made her way over to the bins of DVDs.

'What about this one? She's quite fit!' she shouted over at me. I somehow managed to walk over despite the fact I had never heard a girl conduct herself in such a fashion. The prospect of having a mate who was a lesbian was overwhelmingly exciting.

'Yeah, she's nice' I said eventually, not entirely sure if 'nice' was the kind of word used to describe a girl being spit-roasted.

'What's your type then?' she asked me. It was something I was often asked and had therefore prepared an entire answer for.

'Well Catherine, I wouldn't say I have a type *per se*. There obviously has to be a physical attraction on the surface of it however my type is more of an all round package. You can ascertain a lot more about someone from the way they conduct themselves and the music they listen to than what they look like'.

I thought this was an excellent and democratic response. It had done me well up until this point. I figured it was better than the standard 'I like blondes' which always sounds terribly male chauvinistic.

'Just whatever you can get then right?' she replied, nudging me and laughing.

I wanted to ask what her type was but wasn't entirely sure how I would ever be able to fathom the appropriate response to her answer so just kept quiet. She continued to flick through the stack for a minute more, as though she were merely searching through medical records.

'That's my type' she finally exclaimed, holding a film up, inches from my face. I have to admit Catherine has fantastic taste in women.

She chose however not to buy anything and I have since wondered if the whole activity was just a test to see how comfortable I was around the subject. As soon as we stepped outside, Zara, Dal and Zach started walking off with purpose, as though they had chosen our next destination while we were still inside. It always seemed like decisions were being made for me while I was busy looking at porn.

It was our second and last full day in Amsterdam. I was set on the idea of just chilling out in a café for the afternoon. I had managed to coax everyone into one the previous evening for a quick smoke and had finished the joint that morning but I wasn't satisfied. After all we were in the city I had described as being 'Disneyland for students'.

'I think we should just chill out in a café this afternoon' I suggested to the group.

'I concur' said Zach, who I could always rely upon.

'I still have this tickly cough, so I shan't be smoking' said Zara, clutching a hand to her scarf as though her throat were about to fall off into her hands.

'I could smoke' said Dal, which as it turned out was a massive understatement.

'I won't smoke but I will have a cup of tea and a brownie' said Catherine.

'That's it then' I said, unusually decisively. We changed trajectory and started on the well-worn route to Baba's, the only café I knew of at the time.

As if it emphasise the fact it would be a good idea to clear us from the city streets the winter wind picked up in our faces. We hunched over and with a fresh determination got to the café. Nobody spoke until we were inside, had found a table and placed our orders.

I wasn't satisfied with just having a cup of coffee and a 'special brownie'. Looking beyond the raised countertop I could see rows and rows of pre-rolled joints in coloured test tubes.

The curiosity was too much for me. I needed to know a little more. On a laminated sheet taped to the counter was a price list. I couldn't go alone. I needed my Watson.

'Zach, come with me a minute' I said, throwing myself back out of the deep comfortable chair I had just settled into.

'Ah dude, I just sat down' he replied, getting up regardless of his complaint. We were like kids in a sweet shop. If it were a film the song *Pure Imagination* would have been playing. We gazed up at more variety than we had ever been able to imagine.

On campus the joys of Morrison Haze, Pink Kush and Big Buddha Cheese were something completely alien. Protocol for picking up was to place a call, more often than not to Naz. He would give you a public meeting point and would turn up late to hand over a cling film or silver foil wrap of seeds and stalks. It was all we could get and soon became all we knew. The idea of variety was completely unimaginable. The only comparison I can make is being so poor, as a student, you eat nothing but penne pasta for a month. Then your student loan arrives and you visit a supermarket.

This meant when the moody looking clerk arrived to take our order we were completely lost. The table of names, weights and prices was advanced quantum physics to us.

I also attempted to use some Dutch, to test it out. I assumed because I had a small percentage of Dutch heritage the language would flow from me like tea from a pot. Instead, what I managed to do was speak neither English or Dutch, a language I know one word of; dag (pronounced *dach*), which means goodbye. Zach allowed me to carry on making noises neither party to the proposed transaction could understand for a little too long before he cut in.

'Can...we....have' he said, overdoing and punctuating each word, 'one...yeah, one...joint...you know, smoke, joint, weed… One joint of White Widow…please'.

'One White Widow' she replied in Bond villainess English. In a flash she spun around, collected a red test tube, and placed it between us on the counter.

Somewhat embarrassed we returned to the table, and lit up. It was without a doubt one of the best joints I have ever smoked. It was so good when I later tried to recall the name of the type we had smoked I had to refer to Zach for confirmation.

I have a habit of smoking what Igby Slocumb referred to as 'vegetarian joints', by which I mean they are thin and peppered with crumbled weed. Most people I know load a joint like a revolver. I prefer the slow burn, taking a whole evening to eventually get high, rather than just smoking one to knock you down for the ten count. The joint we had purchased however, was not a vegetarian joint. It was a bleeding steak dinner joint.

For a while I forgot how to speak, and wasn't in the least bit concerned. The whole time we were passing the joint around Zara looked on with disdain, and as it was passed through her personal space; because she was sat between Dal and Zach, she would raise her fist to her mouth and issue a gentle cough as though we were a real danger to her health.

Once I had re-taught myself the entirety of the English language, or at least as much of it as I had previously known, and my one word of Dutch, I was hit with an incredible thirst, as though I had been chewing on an hourglass.

Luckily while we had been smoking the drinks had arrived. I lunged forward and was impressed to find I could still control most of my body. I picked up my coffee and wanted to stay suspended in the moment forever. The taste of the coffee was absolutely incredible. The chocolate and foam that caked the surface bustled on my top lip like a chemical reaction. The heat emitted restored my bones. I wanted to lift up my layers – overcoat, jumper, t-shirt – and show everyone the red glowing light I was certain my belly was giving. From that point it body popped down through my thighs, through my calves, into each of my toes and then poured out the ends, filling my shoes. It was like climbing into a caffeine bath in slow motion.

'Michael, are you okay?' Catherine asked.

I snapped out of the metaphorical bath, wrapped a towel around my midriff and answered the door to the world.

'Yep. Yeah. Cool. I'm fine'.

'It's just everyone was talking and you haven't said a word for quite a while. It's not like you'.

'Oh'.

'Are you sure you're okay?'

'Yeah, I'm just a bit… you know' I said, trying to explain with my hands. I sat up, trying to look as though I were in control and hadn't drifted off to somewhere else entirely while I was being spoken to. I stuck a knife through the middle of the white chocolate chip muffin I had been served, dipped a slab of it into my coffee, and jammed the dripping mixture into my mouth.

'Does everything in here come with weed in it?' I asked.

'Well, the cakes and muffins definitely do. It says so in the menu' Zach replied.

'Yeah, I know that, but what about the toasties?'

'You're asking if they put weed in toasted sandwiches?'

'Yeah', I said. ' Is that so strange?'

'You're fooking out of it dude' said Zach, purposely making himself sound more Manchester than usual to deliver his swear word. He started chuckling at me.

'I'm fine' I said. 'This muffin doesn't even taste like weed'.

'I don't think they are very strong. I'm going to order a brownie as well, just to go with the last of my tea'.

Zach got up and wandered back to the counter. He seemed a lot sturdier on his feet than I assumed I would be if forced to get up and out for some reason. My mind drifted to how I would react if there was some kind of genuine emergency that meant we would have to evacuate the building, maybe a fire alarm. I reasoned there was no way they had a working fire alarm in a café in Amsterdam. I would be perfectly fine.

Zach returned to the table and got to work on his brownie, munching it up, washing it down with a gulp of tea and then repeating the process until his plate just held sticky residue.

'Shall we fook off then?' he asked, still chewing.

We had decided it would be best if we headed back to the hostel we were staying in, to chill out for a while, maybe have a quick nap and then prepare ourselves to go out for dinner to celebrate our last evening in the city of sin. I refused to head back without a secure promise of more White Widow, in case I needed it.

I slowly eased myself to my feet and then, walking as though I were in zero gravity, made it to the counter and bought another red test tube which I slid into the inside pocket of my coat for safekeeping.

Stepping back outside into the bitter wind we followed the route we were only just becoming accustomed to, passing shops on either side and ensuring the canal was always one block to our left. It was the only way we knew how to ensure we got back to the hostel, and our room. We walked through the foyer as one and piled into the cramped lift. Being in such close proximity again reminded me of our shared experience in the peep show booth but the new situation felt so far removed and nobody could make eye contact for fear of laughing in one another's faces.

By the time the lift stopped and we were into our room we were basically dribbling on the floor, carrying ourselves as though the world were on our backs. We collapsed on to our respective beds and took a moment to compose ourselves. It took me about five attempts to get onto my bed because I had called shotgun on the top bunk of one of the two sets of bunk beds we had in the room. No matter how high I jumped, or how many attempts I made I could not convince my arms to straighten out or for my elbows to lock so I could perform the necessary gymnastics. The giggly group high seemed to stretch on forever, until I worried we might never come down, like the scene in *Mary Poppins* where they have afternoon tea on the ceiling.

The main reason we were getting worse rather than better, or coming up rather than returning back down is it takes a little while longer for the weed to hit when it is disguised amongst baked goods. That is why it is always advisable to leave it a good half an hour after eating one before you decide it has had no effect and you need to go back for another. Zach didn't know this. None of us seemed to then. Later I felt it was something I had been informed of previously but for whatever reason hadn't felt it appropriate to mention it at the time.

Unable to deal with what his body was experiencing, Dal excused himself from the room to take a moment to try and stop himself from laughing.

We had reached a point where the laughter had become a form of core exercise. The muscles in my stomach were contracted so tightly I felt I could have been used as a chopping board. The thought made me hungry again, so I rolled off my bed to the floor and started searching through my bags for any kind of snack I could feast upon. Before I could find anything else I found my new hat, a white beanie covered in lime green marijuana leaves and matching tassels.

I had bought it the previous day while high and under the illusion it was the coolest thing in the world, and I thought wearing it would make me the coolest person in the world by association. I put it on. It made me feel a little better. As it happened I did have food perfect for the situation.

We had got to Amsterdam by coach, from Dover to Calais, then through France, Belgium and into Holland. We had stopped at a filling station somewhere along the Belgian motorway and in the fifteen-minute break we were given I had bought two share-size bags of tortilla chips called *Banderos*. One of the bags had survived the journey untouched and I pulled it free from my suitcase. I was so pleased with myself it might as well have been the discovery of a new species. The shout of awe and surprise I emitted was enough to shake everyone from the almost dreams they were entering.

I offered the crisps around but everyone was still full and docile, I couldn't get any takers. Between my offers around the room I scooped up a handful of the snacks and stuffed them into my face. For some reason it seemed hilarious to offer people crisps.

'Zara, do you want some Banderos?' She didn't even look at me, just offered a soft moan. 'Catherine, do you want some Banderos?'

'No' she said. 'How are you still eating? Just lie down'.

Catherine was positioned on her bed, on her front but balanced up on her elbows reading. I never saw the title of the book but swear it must have been *Oranges Aren't The Only Fruit.*

'Zach, do you want some Banderos?'

'No, I want a fooking piss though!' he replied, rolling off his bed in a similar way to me, and padding into the bathroom. I sat cross-legged on the floor and continued to eat my crisps, staring myself out in the mirror that hung on the back of the door. I was unbelievably content. My ears were giving off a faint ringing it had either been too loud to notice before or I had completely ignored. It was eventually cut through by the sound of Zach pissing on the other side of the wall, in the en suite bathroom.

The front door opened and Dal slid back into the room and perched himself on the corner of his bed awkwardly. He had a smug grin spread across his face, inhabiting it. He placed his hands in a heap on his lap and stared at me with hanging eyelids. In years to follow I would grow to know that expression very well, it would become a mascot face for my university experience.

'Where have you been?' I asked.

'Well, I went out into the corridor to calm down, but I could still hear you guys talking and it was still making me laugh so I got into the lift, but then it started moving and some other people got in, and I think I might be paranoid because I swear they were staring at me'.

'Wow, you have had quite the adventure. Would you like some Banderos?' I replied, hoisting the bag up in his face. He ushered it away with a shake of his head.

'Where's Zach?' he asked, noticing the empty bed on his left.

'He's in the toilet' I said absently, swan diving my hand back into the bag for more crisps.

I heard the bolt slide across from the lock in the bathroom followed by the sound of Zach attempting to open the door. There was a pause and then he jiggled the door back and forth in the frame.

'Alright guys' he called from behind the somehow inoperable door. 'I get it. Get off!' Dal and I looked from each other's blank expressions, to the door and then started laughing.

'Dude, we are nowhere near the door' Dal said. He tried it again. It seemed to be stuck fast.

'Not cool guys, just let go of the handle'.

Zara had sat up to try and work out what the noise stopping her from enjoying her catnap was about. Catherine had averted her gaze from her book and was arching her neck to look at the door, which Zach was loudly punching from the other side.

'Zach, calm down!' said Zara. The punching stopped. 'There really is nobody near the door'.

'I'm scared guys!' he said. I wanted to laugh but by judging everyone else's stern expressions I managed to reset my own.

'Are you really trapped?' asked Zara.

'The door won't budge'.

'Right. I'm calling down to reception' she responded, sitting up too quickly. I started to needlessly panic about the joint in my pocket.

'Just open the door!' I said.

'It won't budge', came the muffled response. I really didn't want to get up but it seemed it was the only option available to any of us. I rocked back and forth three times before I built up the momentum to stand, and even then I wasn't particularly steady on my feet. They felt like dead weight, crippled with the beginnings of pins and needles. As I took a step towards the toilet door it leapt forwards and I caught it just before it could clash with my forehead. In one swift movement Zach fell through the door and landed on Dal's bed, narrowly missing taking him out in the process.

'Oh' he said, pulling himself up and attempting to compose. 'I thought it was a pull door!'

I was under the misapprehension I was done with laughter until he said that.

It was ten minutes before I could get the air back in my lungs. I had laughed so much they felt like popped balloons, dangling behind my ribs. Once my breathing had resumed I took the red test tube from my coat, removed the perfectly rolled joint and opened the window.

'You can't smoke that in here. It specifically says this is a *no smoking* hostel' said Zara.

'It's fine. It's Amsterdam, the only law is there are no laws'.

'That's anarchy!' she cried. I lit the joint and inhaled deeply, melodramatically.

'Do you want some of this?' I asked around the room. I don't think any of them could have stood to smoke it even if they wanted to. They just looked completely out of it. I still had further to dissolve though. I wanted to make the most of it.

I managed about half of the joint before I started to feel a rising kind of sickness. One of the key things Dad always taught me was when the room starts spinning it is time to stop. Nothing good can come from trying to go beyond that point, it is always best to just take cover and ride out the storm. I stubbed the remainder out on the window ledge, returned it to the test tube and crawled into bed.

I awoke too many hours later in a daze. My tongue was soldered to the roof of my mouth and any sense of taste had evaded me. My eyes were stuck with sleep glue and the harsh overhead lighting in the room was not my friend.

I could make out the sound of running water, but dismissed it as being rain drumming like fingertips on the windowpane. I sat up suddenly and realised where I was, hovering five foot off the floor above a sleeping lesbian. I dragged my long body up and peered over the edge. Catherine was nowhere to be seen. Somehow she had managed to disappear from under me as I slept.

That wile lesbian I thought to myself.

I looked out over the room. Zach was face down on his bed, arms and legs spread like a starfish. He was still completely out of it. Zara was curled up like a sleeping mouse, her arms huddled around her rucksack. Dal was asleep with his hands just before his mouth, almost clenched in prayer.

The sound of the running water cut abruptly with a squeak. I realised it was the shower. The door to the bathroom opened and Catherine stepped out, a towel wrapped just around the top of her cleavage and her hair piled up high on her head.

I dropped back onto my bunk and pretended to be asleep. She carefully tiptoed over to our bed. I could hear the soft sucking sound of her wet feet on the dusty plastic floor. Watching through almost down lids I saw her check around the room and then with her back to me she quickly dropped her towel to the floor. I managed to oppress the gasp that began to snowball up from the depths of my throat.

That moment taught me something I had spent far too long thinking about. It is often the case when a straight woman learns an aesthetically agreeable man is gay they will utter the phrase 'oh, such a waste'. I never really understood the meaning behind it. The first example I can think of is George Michael, who I have in the past heard my own mother declare a fancy for. I feel I should specify she was talking about *Faith* era George, not 'drunken car crash into a Snappy Snaps' George. I never really understood exactly what it meant. It doesn't matter whether a man is gay or straight, you should still be able to appreciate the beauty they hold. I was of that belief until Catherine dropped her towel and I caught sight of what we, as a gender, were missing out on.

Oh, what a waste!

I was flat against the bed and not in the most comfortable position. I felt I had to wait until she was in a reasonable state of dress before I dared move in case she realised I had been watching the whole parade, and there was a very good reason for her preferring women, and that it was because men are objectifying pigs.

I closed my eyes under the pretence it would provide her with some kind of dignity. I listened carefully to her drying off. With my eyes squeezed shut my hearing was amplified.

Next came the elastic of her underwear with a snap against her smooth thighs. I heard the ruffle of a bra being clipped and turned before the straps were pulled up. I listened to her pulling her skinny jeans back on and then I let out the biggest, most exaggerated yawn known to man to prepare her for my pretend arrival into consciousness.

'Morning sleepyhead' she called from beneath me. 'You say some weird things in your sleep, don't you?'

'Do I?' I asked, lifting my head from the mattress I hadn't realised I had been digging it into.

'Yeah, it was something about a crocodile and the sunshine'.

'Oh yeah. Don't worry about that'.

She stood up, and in the same movement pulled a vest top over her exposed flesh, closing it off from me forever. It felt safe to sit up.

'What time is it?' I asked.

'Getting on for nine'.

'Shit, did we sleep right through?'

'No Michael, it's 9pm'.

'Oh okay, I don't think anyone was planning on sleeping for that long'.

'Should we wake them up?'

'I don't know if that is cool. Maybe we should just make a bit of noise' I said.

'Okay, but be-'.

Before Catherine could finish her sentence I launched my pillow across the room where it landed flat on Zach's back.

'Wake up dinkus!' I called. He sat up straight away, as though he had been waiting for it. I wondered if he had watched Catherine get changed as well. Within seconds Dal was upright, massaging the sides of his head, and Zara was sliding the sleep from her eyes with the side of her hand.

'Are we going out then, or what?' asked Zach.

'Yeah, of course' said Zara. 'What time is it?'

'Nine' I said.

'Did we sleep straight through?' she asked.

'No Zara, it's 9pm' I said, employing the same sarcastic tone Catherine had used on me.

With a very brief check in the mirror we all headed back out onto the streets. By that point we were not particularly concerned if our last night in Amsterdam was a big one or not. We were just hoping the grooves we had heated and worn into the mattress would be there upon our return.

****

I awoke the following morning with a handshake like carbon monoxide. I struggled to work out where I was. The paint flakes skipping from the wall were not my own. The smells were not my own. Even the cold in the air felt different to what I knew. My head pumped with the memories of the previous night. I struggled to place myself, to try and work out exactly what had happened to put me in such a state of misunderstanding. It came back in slabs, like meat on hooks in an abattoir. I buzzed around it like a fly before I could get anything.

A seedy looking rat man hunched in a doorway.

Rummaging through shelves.

Another smoke before bedtime.

I tried to recall exactly what had happened.

I remembered oversleeping from our naps and deciding we would go out for dinner. Given the time it proved somewhat more difficult than we had anticipated and we settled into a pizzeria not far from the hostel. It wasn't the most Dutch meal imaginable but all the food I had eaten in Amsterdam seemed to be junk. The only thing my old man had ever taught me about Dutch cuisine was they put mayonnaise on chips instead of ketchup.

Running low on money I had settled for a cheese and tomato pizza and a side of tap water. I then had to deal with everyone else eating the most lavish items on the menu.

After dinner we rolled around the streets of Amsterdam not entirely sure what to do with ourselves. If I had the money I would have considered getting a prostitute, not necessarily to have sex with, just to alleviate the boredom, and for the anecdote. I feel I should state now I have never paid for sex. Not directly.

I would probably have chickened out and just wanted to talk like Holden Caulfield did. I felt we had already had our fill of Saturday night in Amsterdam. I wished our naps had just extended through to the morning. It might have been due to the laziness smoking always seemed to impose upon me.

As we walked past the lit up red glow windows of beautiful European girls a creepy rodent man emerged from the shadows and cooed at Zach and I.

'Want to see a sex show?'

'Already seen one mate' replied Zach as we kept walking.

'Not like this you haven't'.

While we were tempted by his alluring comment we were stony broke. We didn't have the money to go and watch any foreign object, be it banana, ping-pong ball or Twix enter an orifice.

When the man realised he wasn't going to get any business from us he turned on the girls who were following in our elongated shadow.

'Girls, how about coming and seeing a big cock for once!'

Zach and I just laughed. The idea we were *with* the girls was completely insane and the way business could be touted in such a fashion was so far removed from the stiff upper lip of our British ways. It was the first and only time I haven't been offended by someone insulting my manhood.

It was something of an awakening for us all. I would like to romanticise the whole affair and compare it to when The Beatles lived in Hamburg, working as a house band in seedy bars, cruising around the red light district and experimenting with drink and drugs. It was the period before they returned home to start claiming the world as their own.

'I tell you what' said Zach, 'let's see who can find the most fucked up porno in these shops'. I was completely ready. It was a game we could play without spending a penny. It also wouldn't involve exhorting too much energy. One of my natural states of being is perusing DVDs. Here it was not just as an activity, but a challenge.

'Anal?' said Zach, plucking the first disc in reach from a shelf.
'Beat it! Double penetration!'
'Anal fisting'.
'Bukkake!'
'That's not worse'.
'I'm never eating a cake you've iced then'.
'That's what your Mum said'.
'Animals?'
'Yeah, that's pretty sick. What animal?'
'A dog'.
'I've found one with a horse'.

There are limits even within the porn world and we soon exhausted our sources. There was nothing left to do but head back out into the cold.

'Is it wrong I sort of want to just go back, have a joint and pass out?' I asked.

'No dude, why didn't you say? That's just what I want to do'.

'You're not smoking in that room. I have to sleep in there, and I have a cold' piped in Zara who we had all but forgotten about.

'We will have the window open. You won't even notice' said Zach. Before she could respond he ran off into a weird looking café on the corner of the street we had found ourselves on. We wanted White Widow, we had developed a taste for it, like dogs being passed leftovers under the table.

'I feel sick' said Zara suddenly. She started off after Zach before we could go after her, with the far removed intention of finding a toilet to hover over and vomit into.

Somehow their paths did not cross and Zach emerged completely unaware Zara was even missing.

'Are we going back then? They didn't have any Widow so I had to get Trainwreck'.

'Zara isn't feeling well' said Catherine.

'Ooh, what's Trainwreck!' I asked.

'So?' Zach replied, staring at Catherine. I watched the jet of condensation leave his mouth spitefully. It made me realise how cold it was. I pulled the lapels of my coat in. Dal stayed quiet for the duration, hovering on the periphery.

'We have to wait for her' Catherine said, pointing back in the direction Zach had walked towards us from.

'I want to smoke though' he said with a whine. 'She knows the way back. It'll be fine'.

'No, we aren't going anywhere, just wait a minute'.

I wondered if Zara could have been pregnant. It was always the first thought that came to mind when any girl was being sick. I think too many episodes of *Grange Hill* and *Byker Grove* had altered my perception and lodged in my subconscious.

I tried to work out who she had *been with* recently. I knew she had a fiancé but on campus that wasn't conclusive of anything, in the same way what you chose to study had no meaning. I had been to nursing lectures.

Zara eventually emerged, looking paler than her usual ginger pallor allowed. Catherine put her arm across Zara's shoulders and we marched her back to the hostel, flanking her on all sides like raggedy bouncers.

Once we were back in the room Zach had lost none of the focus he had exhibited during Zara's disappearing and vomiting act. We were going to smoke that joint regardless of how other people were feeling.

Catherine put Zara to bed and she curled up under the covers, looking pathetic and falling asleep almost instantly. It was just the excuse we needed. Someone took a towel and placed it along the bottom of the door that led into the hallway. While I was sure the majority of people smoked in their rooms the guilt stuck to my skin like sweat. The four of us gathered around the window and passed the joint once before Catherine concluded she'd had enough. She settled onto her bunk and was asleep before the boys had finished the rest. We stumbled off to rest up for the next day, and the return journey.

As I said, I awoke the following morning with a handshake like carbon monoxide. I struggled to work out where I was, and why I was. I rolled over and looked out over the room, experiencing an odd sense of déjà vu. It was travel day.

We had until lunchtime to get the last bits of naughtiness from our systems before we boarded the coach to take us back the way we had come, through

Holland, Belgium and France, to the ferry, and then home.

Everyone showered quickly, packed their stuff and we eloped to Baba's to ride out the last few hours. It felt as though we had been away for a lot longer than the two nights we had been afforded. It was as though we had completed some incredible trek across to another land in search of ourselves, time rammed up like a pile up on a motorway. I wasn't completely aware of my body, everything felt distant and fuzzy as though I had been numbed ready for the operating theatre.

I just ordered a cup of tea because I couldn't stomach the thought of anything else. Nobody else seemed as concerned about my constitution. They ordered cakes and toasted sandwiches. I couldn't focus on any of it, and just tried to watch my hand for long enough that it would stop shaking.

'The best thing you can do dude' said Zach, spitting bits of brownie at me between mouthfuls, 'the best thing you can do is just get high as balls'.

'Why?' I asked, wrapping both my earthquake-ridden hands around the mug of tea.

'That way, you can sleep the whole way home. You won't even think about it. You will just wake up on campus. It will feel like a dream'.

It seemed like a brilliant idea. Zach had already gone to the trouble of buying us another joint. He had gone for some kind of Haze because variety is the spice of life. He lit up and we smoked it between us. For some reason Dal chose this moment to get up and wander off. I assumed he just needed some fresh air because he had overindulged the previous evening. I was corrected when he walked in, munching a Carroll-esque mushroom.

'Where did you get that?' Zach asked him, performing a double take at the fungi.

'Down the road. I figured you are right. We need to sleep through the journey home. I thought I would give magic mushrooms a try'.

'Dude, have you not had mushrooms before?'

'No. Why?'

'Well, I hate to be the one to tell you this' Zach lied, 'but they don't work like that'.

'I'll be fine' Dal replied and stuffed the rest into his mouth.

It was about half an hour before things started to get strange, and by 'things' I mean Dal. It was just as Zara decided to stop feeling sorry for herself and join in with the conversation. The reason for her sudden change in temperament was the imminent departure of the coach. She was a sucker for organising other people about.

'Come on guys, don't want to miss our ride home' she said, clapping her hands together. We all got up, moaning about how comfortable and warm we had been, and dreading the twelve-hour coach journey ahead of us. The only one who didn't move was Dal, who remained still, arms stretched along the length of his high-backed leather chair.

'Come on Dal' she said.

'I'll be out in a minute. I've just got to find something' he replied. At first it sounded like a completely normal and acceptable sentence so we picked up our stuff and headed outside to wait for him, so we could all pile on the coach together.

After five minutes we realised Dal might have been having some issues and it would probably be best for someone to return into the café to help him with whatever the problem seemed to be. Somehow I was nominated to be that someone.

When I pushed the door to Baba's open once more I could see Dal in the far corner, hunched over his open suitcase. He was hurriedly searching through it, picking up piles of clothes, dumping them on the lid and running his fingers around the inner edges of it's lined interior as though he were looking for loose change in a pocket.

'Dal' I said, approaching slowly, like he was a dangerous beast. 'What are you doing?'

'I'm looking for *something*' he said. The way he uttered the word *something* really struck me. It sounded loaded.

'Well, what is it?' I asked.

'*Something*'.

'Yeah. If you don't tell me what it is then I can't help you look for it can I?' I replied, half-laughing.

He turned on me suddenly, with venom and snarl.

'I told you, I'm looking for *something*!'

He said it so loud the room went silent. There was nothing else going on. I felt I needed a wooden chair in my arm to keep him at a safe distance. It clicked for me. Mushrooms did funny things to people. Zach had been completely right, he had foreseen the incident. Dal's pupils were so far dilated I could see my approaching reflections in the black depths. They were like Rorschach tests. I realised the only way to get him out was to speak on his level. I had an insight into the deranged mind.

'You're looking for *something*' I said, keeping careful emphasis on employing the same pronunciation and tone of the word as he had. I wanted to mirror him exactly.

'Yeah' he said, concluding his search and beginning the entire process again. The problem was the object Dal was searching for was not going to be found. It wasn't even an object. It was the concept. He was quite literally searching for 'something' as though it were an object he could own, hold, or possess.

I thought my options through. I had dealt with people in all kinds of states of duress as a result of drug-related delusions. All he really needed was someone to take charge. If that wasn't what he needed he could always murder me with a teaspoon.

I quickly reached forward and pulled the suitcase shut. Dal pulled his hands back at the last second. I zipped the case closed and stood it upright.

'There. Everything is in there. Let's go and get the coach'. His eyes flared for a moment before softening back to reality. He blinked away the paranoia.

'Okay' he replied, and gentle as a lamb got up so I could lead him back outside and onto the waiting coach.

Aboard the bus there were two televisions, one at the front above the driver and one in the middle above the stairs to the toilets. Zach had managed to secure us the best seats, just in front of the central TV. They had slightly more legroom, and we could bask in the seemingly warm glow of the television.

I took the window seat for the first part of the journey. I pulled my sweatshirt off and used it as a makeshift pillow. Whenever I looked out at the city, which seemed so calm and beautiful when the sun was up, I could also make out a pale, clammy version of myself reflected in the glass. I looked like Banquo's ghost.

All I wanted was vegetables and sleep. I realised I was just as tweaked as Dal. We had ventured beyond the looking glass and were happy to be returning to a world where no matter how strange things got there was always a sense of rationality to it. Amsterdam did not make sense to me.

I fell asleep in the flashing lights from the TV. *Lucky Number Slevin* was playing. I awoke just in time for the plot twist.

I drifted in and out of focus as Zach had promised. It wasn't until we got to Calais I came to a stark realisation. I still had a red test tube in my pocket containing half a joint. The bus was pulled in at the port and we were ordered to get off and present our passports.

I had two options. I could either jam the plastic cone up my arse and know I would probably make it through or I could keep it in my pocket and hope they were not performing searches or had dogs on patrol.

I won't say which I chose; I wouldn't want you to judge me.

The Devillenerve Sisters

MICHAEL
October 2006

'Come on! It's not like you have anything better to do tonight!'

That was the line that did it. It was the line that led to the night I met someone who would have more of an effect over my life than I feel comfortable admitting.

I was sat on the bottom step of the lower half of the stairs of the flat. I had just begun my second year of studies having scraped through my exams, and was living in St John's Halls Of Residence with Harry and Sophie.

On the banister beside me were their initials, scratched into the varnish. They were in love and it meant I couldn't drag Harry off to a party because he would have his night planned, turning in early and making wild, loud love which reverberated through the paper-thin walls into my own room where I sat night after night rocking back and forth to the rhythm, lost in my own loneliness.

My best hope of getting any sleep I concluded, was to go to Zach's as he had been insisting to me on the phone, and return home drunk once the whole sordid business was over with. I switched the headset across to my right ear, catching it expertly between my head and shoulder and reaching into the pocket of my shorts for a lighter.

I let Zach continue to talk as I relit the rolled cigarette clenched between my lips. I let him continue despite the fact I had made my decision.

'You have to come because I can't deal with Zara's new boyfriend on my own' Zach said, all tinny and northern through the receiver. 'He's one of those Topman trendy types. He doesn't have a clue about music. We can drink some beers, play some music and maybe they'll just fook off'.

'They? You mean Zara and.... What's his name?'

'Ross. He's Ross but there's another one. He's bringing a friend'.

'Who?' I asked cautiously.

'I don't know. Another first year, they're all the same to me. You need to come over to stop me starting a fight with them'.

Despite how Manchester he may have seemed, Zach was not one for fighting.

'I will come, but I'm not fighting, and I want a safety word'.

'What for?'

'In case it gets too much and I want to leave. I want a word I can say and you will know straight away I need to get out of there'.

'What about *beer*?'

'Dude. We are definitely going to say beer'.

'Okay then. If you say *mediocre*'.

'Why would I say that?'

'Because you're a soft southern shandy!'

He had a point. I am. I looked down to where my cigarette had gone out, resting between the first and second fingers of my left hand.

'Are we going to the bar?'

'Nah. Just staying at mine. Don't dress up or anything'.

I didn't. I walked over to St Christopher's where Zach and Zara lived in my *Cajun Dance Party* t-shirt, skinny jeans, green Converse and a military jacket I had bought the previous Summer in an army surplus store which somehow made me look like an apprentice postman.

Zach opened the door and ushered me in. He was in his usual uniform of black skinny jeans, check Vans and a black t-shirt promoting a band I didn't like. His hair was fluffier than usual.

'They're here already' he said, motioning down the hall with a sneer. 'They're in the kitchen'.

He was talking as though his kitchen were occupied by Nazis. As much as there were plenty of arseholes on campus, and many of them I had the misfortune of knowing, I was yet to reach a point where I instantly dismissed anyone new.

'Is Zara in there?' I asked.

'Yeah, of course she is'.

I heard laughter from the kitchen. Three separate laughs joining up like drops of blood on fabric.

'Just come in my room for five minutes'.

I followed Zach into his room. It was completely covered in posters, the majority of which were of *emo* bands. They all had big dyed-black fringes and eyeliner and from their poses looked menacing, camp or a confusing mix of both. Each time I looked at them, I couldn't help but wince. As a bassist Zach was strong, so I overlooked our differences in musical taste. He could hold his own and play along with anything I wrote for us to jam to.

My white Fender Stratocaster copy was leaning against the edge of his desk like The Fonz. It lived there. I made a dive for it. I felt a lot more natural when I had a guitar on my lap, between me and people. It was a defence.

'I have a new album for you to listen to' Zach said once I was settled on the edge of his bed.

'Oh, who is it this time?'

'I'm not saying because you'll judge it and you shouldn't do that. Just listen to it because it's fooking genius'.

He sat at his desk, at his computer and once it had jumped to life he started the album. Straight away I hated it and I knew we were going to have an argument about it. I didn't want to be difficult and I wasn't looking for trouble. I'm just very particular about music. I sat patiently and waited for the whole awful business to come to a close.

'Well' he said.

'I can see why you like it'.

'How very fooking democratic of you' he said, and got up to head into the kitchen, obviously concluding it was better to spend the evening with them than try to teach me about the intricacies of *AFI*'s work. I followed in his wake.

As we neared the end of the corridor there was a fresh bout of laughter. I worried it was at our expense, a reflex I had held since childhood.

'Michael, this is my boyfriend' Zara said as we entered. I made a move to reach across the table to shake his hand. He raised half out of his plastic chair in order to meet me in the middle.

'Ross' he said, as though connecting with a tribesman who had never encountered civilisation.

'Alright. I'm Michael' I said back, despite the fact Zara had literally just used my name. I wasn't sure what I made of him in those first few seconds. As I went to take a seat his friend stood to greet me. I felt suddenly overwhelmed, as though I were about to be crushed to death under a bookcase. At my spindly six foot it was rare I made contact with anyone who made me feel like a small boy again but Oliver Bannatyne did just that.

It wasn't that he was inches taller than me. He was also wide. Not in any way that could be described as stocky or chubby, despite his insistence he was fat years down the line. He was just broad, and full, like a man, whereas I still had the wiry torso of a boy. His hair was expertly matted and teased and there was a wry grin on his lips. I practically fell backwards like Sarah Connor at the sight of him.

'Alright mate' he said, offering up a hand for me to shake or hang off of. 'I'm Oliver'.

'Michael' I replied, placing my hand in his where it got lost.

'I like your jacket' he said.

'Thanks' I replied.

'Do you want a beer?'

'Yes please'.

He passed me a beer and I sat down, concluding anyone who offers up a beer within the first thirty seconds of meeting them can't be all bad. It wasn't what I had been expecting at all. When Zach told me they were first year students I imagined spotty awkward little boys trying to impress and make friends with everyone they came into contact with. Oliver was quite different. He seemed so self-assured and confident.

Zach sat in the corner with a face like an incoming storm. The exact impact Oliver had on me during our first meeting was near enough the opposite of how I immediately felt about Ross. I wanted to sit and relax and pretend there wasn't anything concerning me but it just isn't my way. It's hard to be calm when someone is wearing a rhinestone Rolling Stones t-shirt. It was the glittering elephant in the room and I couldn't feel comfortable until I had mentioned it. It was like a mirror ball. Anywhere else I looked I could see it refracting, bouncing off faces and objects. I had to settle the matter.

'You like the Rolling Stones then?'

I couldn't help it. It's a problem. I know I have issues. Ross looked down at his shirt and seemed genuinely surprised to find it attached to his body.

'Oh. Yeah?' he replied.

I knew it. He had no real interest in the Stones. It annoyed me music had become a fashion thing. Bands like The Ramones and Rolling Stones were being used to sell all kinds of unrelated shit. I had spent years of school being bullied for being into grunge and suddenly it was cool and fashionable. I'm not saying I invented a scene, far from it. I was always a follower, but it was legitimate.

Not only did I conclude Ross wasn't musically educated. I knew he would only know one Stones song.

'What's your favourite song?' I asked.

'*Paint It Black*' he said automatically.

I fucking knew it I thought.

'Oh yeah. That's cool' I said. I took a sip of my beer knowing I had checkmated the scenester fad prick bastard. In the same move I tarred Oliver with the same brush, through association alone. I assumed he had just as little a clue about anything.

I appreciate it may seem a lot to conclude from one guy wearing a t-shirt but a lot of who I am is defined by what I wear, so I feel it is necessary to draw the same conclusions about other people.

'Name another song' said Oliver suddenly.

'What?' said Ross.

'Name another Rolling Stones song'.

'Erm...'

'Thought so' said Oliver, and took a victory sip of his beer.

I felt I had found an ally, a kindred spirit to side with in tough times. A lighthouse when the storm suddenly got rough.

'Don't get me wrong' continued Oliver, turning to me and Zach, 'I barely know any Stones songs, but I wouldn't wear their t-shirt for that express reason. I would hate to look like a prick when someone called me out over it'.

Ross squirmed in his chair and started to shrink under our collective gaze.

'He only knows Paint It Black from playing *Guitar Hero* as well' concluded Oliver.

I felt rightfully smug. It was as though I had identified the murderer during the opening scene of an episode of *Murder, She Wrote*.

'Who do you like then?' I asked, testing Oliver further.

'I'm really into Kaiser Chiefs at the moment' he replied. It was better than pretending to like the Stones. I had gone off Kaiser Chiefs as soon as *I Predict A Riot* started getting commercial radio play. Before long it was being covered by every pub band going and used as background music for football coverage.

'Oh yeah, cool. Me too' I said.

I was hoping he could be my musical soulmate. Musical soulmates are very hard to come by.

'What about you?' he asked. I was completely taken aback. I felt so appreciated. Zach gave an exaggerated sigh. He knew I was lost in conversation already.

'Babyshambles at the moment, Dirty Pretty Things, We Are Scientists…'

I continued to list bands, trying to hit some kind of common ground. A point where he would stop me and say 'oh wow, let's be BFF's!'

It didn't happen straight away. I like to believe it was a key point in our friendship though, we viewed each other with a renewed respect. I had established he wasn't to be taken under the umbrella of freshers, and he had realised I wasn't as much of a wanker as I looked.

The important thing to note was something took place, which would set us up as friends for a long time to come. To this day I can only remember snapshots of the conversations we had. We realised we both loved Converse, Kevin Smith films and had an unnatural ability to disappear off on some kind of tenuous link involving a point of pop culture so obscure we would struggle to recall the conversation which had brought us to that point initially. All I can remember with any certainty is the sound of laughter and beer cans opening. To me it was like a joining of forces. It was so strange to find someone so attuned to the way I thought about things, and the jokes I would make. On review it feels as though we completely dominated the evening as a duo and I'm afraid that hasn't really let up since.

It was like going speed dating and realising you had struck gold with the first person you sat opposite. There was something so immediate about it. We could have disappeared off into the bushes together giggling.

It was an hour or so later we started to get a bit giddy and in the mood to cause trouble. Zara had disappeared into her bedroom to speak to one of her friends from home who was suffering some kind of personal crisis. With our captor absent, our boyish nature took over and we started running back and forth in the hall, trying to run up the walls and kicking cans of spit and foam at each other.

Fearing he didn't have enough of the attention because of my fledgling relationship with Oliver, Ross decided to show off. With a righteous belch he ripped down the stuffed heart hung on Zara's door, and started kicking it along the floor. When this didn't draw our gaze he took it into the communal bathroom and threw it in the toilet. Then he dropped his jeans to his ankles and proceeded to urinate on it. This was all of course done with the door wide open.

We left it there for Zara to discover and headed back into the kitchen to talk about things none of us could remember or care about the following morning.

When she emerged from her room Zara seemed even more highly strung than usual. A point exacerbated when she went to relieve her bladder and found the fluffy heart her ex fiancé had given her on the previous Valentine's Day, when he had roared onto campus on his motorbike, under the belief he was in *Grease 2*.

After a few too many beers I decided it was time to head back to my own flat. I didn't want to overdo it, not because I had lectures the following morning, but because I didn't want to make a tit of myself in front of my new friend.

'Night guys' I said, finally picking up my jacket and wavering slightly in the doorway.

'Michael. Where are you walking to?' Oliver asked.

'Oh, I live in St John's, over the other side'.

'Cool. My flat is over there too. I'll come with you'.

We got outside and I shuddered against the inevitable cold that clings to everything after midnight. Oliver looked at me and for a moment I thought he was going to offer me his coat to keep warm.

'I do honestly really like that jacket' he said.

'Oh, okay. Thanks' I said.

'I wasn't just fucking flirting with you or anything. I have one quite similar'.

'Cool'.

We started on our way back to our side of campus.

'I've got about seven pairs of Converse with me as well' he added. I wasn't sure if he was trying to impress me or if we were just struggling to continue the conversation now there was nobody else around to laugh at our jokes, our mutual friends.

'How do you know Ross then?' I asked to keep things moving.

'Oh, he was the first person I met on campus'.

'Really?'

'Yeah. Do you have that one guy?'

'What do you mean?' I asked.

'Sort of a friend, but someone you feel obligated to look after'.

'Sort of a friend?'

'Well, as an example, who was the first person you met on campus?'

'Pingu' I said.

'Pingu?'

'Yeah. He's a DJ'.

'Of course he is. Everyone is a DJ on this campus'.

'I think that goes for most universities'.

'Probably'.

We got to the top of the path where the flats continued around the back. Sticking to the road we headed down, past the gym and towards our eventual resting point.

'I do have one friend like that actually' I said, 'it's sort of like one of those situations where you're trying to work out how you ended up being someone's babysitter'.

'Exactly!'

'But you don't get paid, and you don't get a handjob on their sofa'.

Oliver immediately started laughing and I realised what I had said.

'No! Not off the kid you're babysitting. I mean, like when a girl would come over and then after the kid goes to bed....'

'Yeah, whatever you paedophile!'

'I'm not, I swear'.

'I'm messing about Michael'.

'Oh good, because I would never'.

'Yeah, I know'.

It would be a while before our conversation delved back onto such heavy topics. When we did discuss seedy topics our friendship and conversation was like a heavy object thrown overboard, sinking into the inky depths of the ocean.

'Do you like football?' he asked eventually.

I dreaded being asked, especially when it was by someone I liked. It was a couple of years on from this conversation before I felt comfortable enough to tell people outright I had no interest in the 'beautiful game'. I think the money given to professional footballers should be capped, and given to charity, or to nurses, or to soldiers, people who actually do something with a purpose. It makes absolutely no difference to me whether a football team does well or not. It is completely off my radar.

'Yeah, I played when I was younger' I half lied, through gritted teeth'.

'What's your team?'

'Arsenal'. Again, a half lie.

'No way, me too'.

Fuck I thought. The scenario I found myself in was worse than someone stating another team as their preference, and then jabbering on about how Arsenal weren't the team they had been a couple of seasons before, or how they never should have sold what's-his-name or changed their kit or trained on Astroturf one Wednesday afternoon or whatever else it is people who like football choose to talk about.

'Yeah?' I said.

'Yeah. Haven't been up to the Emirates this season though. What about you?'

I couldn't lie anymore. I had built enough relationships on lies to know it wasn't a good idea, especially with a member of the same sex.

'I went in February 1998 I think'.

'What?'

'That was the last time I went to see them. That was the last time it was any good, you know, with winning the double and everything'.

He looked at me blankly, trying to establish if I was having him on.

'You're right' he eventually said laughing. 'You probably got out at the best time'.

'To tell you the truth I don't really care for football much anymore' I said, stopping completely to exaggerate my point.

'So...' he said, turning back to me. 'Are we walking or are you just going to stand about waiting to be abducted?'

'Both'.

As it happened our flats were very close, in the way only campus accommodation could allow people to live in such close proximity. The back of my flat very nearly faced the front of his. There was going to be no escaping each other, regardless of our wishes.

'You can probably see me in my kitchen from your window' Oliver said.

'I guess so'.

'Dash up there now and I'll put a little show on for you while I cook myself a Pot Noodle'.

'Alright. I will'.

'It was nice to meet you Michael'.

'It was nice to meet you too Oliver'.

We paused. There was just the static of the night as we stared each other out dumbly. We later discussed this and realised usually when you walk someone home there is usually an invitation for coffee, which obviously turns into a fuck. There was no way that would happen on this occasion. We had only just met. We weren't sluts.

'Right, I'll see you around' he said, breaking the moment and walking off.

'I'll see you from my window' I said, and then scurried inside realising it was probably the creepiest thing I could have possibly replied.

When I got upstairs I noticed I could indeed see straight into the kitchen of Oliver's flat. I rolled a cigarette in the light of the moon and watched as the light flashed on and he sauntered in. He waved across the space despite the fact he couldn't tell which window I was at in the darkness. I watched him boil the kettle, make his food, chuck a bunch of dirty plates in the sink and then disappear back to his room, turning off the light after him and leaving me to my thoughts and my smoke.

Afterword

I suppose I may have glamorised or romanticised the whole evening and our first meeting to a certain extent. That is as close as I can recall to the evening I met my friend, and it is a story I struggled with because it isn't the most incredible thing to ever happen to two people. I mean, we didn't die in each other's arms. We didn't drive off a cliff together on the run from the law. We didn't get raped over the bonnet of a 106 together. It just was what it was.

The reason I remember it is it spawned one of the most important friendships of my adult life. I remember on our first day on campus we were invited to an orientation type introduction in the main hall, a room I would enter only a few times in the three years I was on campus. Sometimes it was for an exam but in my first year I made a habit of going there for nursing lectures, a point alluded to earlier in this collection. I used it as an opportunity to chat up girls, and maybe learn a bit of first aid. To this day I can recite the different layers of the skin, and I know how to handle someone suffering an epileptic fit. I also had it off with a number of nursing students so my education was not a complete loss.

The important thing about that first day in the hall was the Dean gave a speech in front of the three hundred or so fresh-faced students and he said something I will never forget. He told us the majority of us would meet the person we would marry during our time at university. It was a sure statistic. He said we could be sat in the room with the person we are going to spend the rest of our lives with.

At this point, Harry turned to Zara, who through coincidence was sat beside us and just said one word:
'Gutted!'

Little did Harry know the woman he was destined to marry was still at home, intending starting her nursing course in our second semester.

I didn't meet the person I would marry at university but I did make a lot of friends who have stuck by me. They have seen me at my worst, and held me through it. They have seen me at my best, and congratulated me for it. There are some who have slightly slipped out of focus but who are very much held in mind. There is however one person who I speak to every day. One person who keeps up with every step of my life and has done so for the last five years. I've told Oliver things I just don't think I could tell anyone else and he has done the same with me. We problem solve for each other. We celebrate our achievements together. It's one of the best and most balanced friendships I've ever had. He is one of the few people I feel can truly understand me and I am pleased things aligned in a certain way and we met, because I'm a lot richer for the experience.

The Curse Of Iggy Sutcliffe

IGGY
June 2007

After a while of sitting there I started to just get really bored. There really is only so long you can sit waiting for anything and I was uncomfortable enough as it was. I felt itchy. My old man had insisted I put a tie on 'for appearance's sake'. It gave me the appearance of being a sweaty mess. The whole thing was so stupid anyway. It's not like they could have thrown me out even if they wanted to. I was that campus! I took the piece of paper I had folded in half and then half again out of my pocket for what must have been the fiftieth time. I was expected to read it's contents to the most important people on campus, aside from me and the football lads obviously, and I felt a bit nervous.

My belly had taken a funny turn and I considered my Dad's sole piece of advice I remembered from childhood, 'when in doubt, go and sit on the toilet'. It had got me through many a rough time. The reason I had been called up was I was fantastically failing my Business Studies course and it wasn't the first time. I don't really feel like going into that because it's very complicated and definitely not my fault. The important thing to note is what was about to happen was very important to my future.

I couldn't get kicked out, I just couldn't. It would mean the end of me. I had been promised a partnership in my Dad's business; a janitorial supplies company, if I came home to Preston with a degree he could proudly hang on the office walls or in the downstairs loo. I started reading through the speech I had prepared but it didn't grab me in the way it had before, when I had written it. I hadn't really thought about my target audience, which is a clever marketing term for the audience you are targeting with your product. It read more like I was talking to the boys. It was rousing but it was more suited to a night on the lash than to a bunch of suited and booted queers. I had to rethink it on the spot.

There were a million things I loved about campus. I loved the fact you couldn't go anywhere without people knowing who you were, and asking what you were doing, and you could go in the bar and your mates would be in there, it was guaranteed. I loved the fact there were so many fit birds about, and that they were all game for a giggle. I loved how the place smelt really nice when the grass had all been cut every other Tuesday morning. I liked how you could fancy dress as a schoolboy or as an army guy and it wasn't seen as being abnormal. I loved the facilities. We had a pool and a gym. I hadn't spent much time in either but the fact they were there was always nice.

Just as I was lost in my own thoughts of all the things I liked, the door opened and a little scrawny woman's face popped out like a vacuum cleaner coming round a bend. Her glasses were balanced on the tip of her big nose and the gold chain they were attached to jangled with the movements.

'Ian, we'll see you now'.

Nobody called me Ian, except Mum, and that was when I was in trouble. I filed in. It was a daunting sight, or it would have been for anyone not as taken with public speaking as how I was. I hosted the pub quiz on a Sunday in Bar One as well as giving several presentations to my class. In the room, which amazed me every time I went into it because of the impressive old school décor, was a big long desk with five or six old men and women behind it. They all had glasses on and suits and that. I had to win them over and I only had a couple of minutes and I knew it.

I stood as far back as I could, assessing my audience.

'Thank you for coming along Ian, now your father-'.

'I don't wish to take up any more of the counsel's time than is entirely necessary' I said, turning on my public voice and stepping forward with a clap of my big hands. 'I did write a proposal for submission and your noble approval however I now believe it counterbalances the intentions of the project. With your blessed say so I wish to exacerbate the move into dynamic retribution by speaking from the ventricles'.

'Mr. Sutcliffe, are you saying your speech is not in fact written, which is essentially an admission on your part of not being able to meet yet another deadline, which is one of the many reasons you find yourself in your current position?'

I stumbled. They had got past my back four and were heading for the box. I had to rethink and defend.

'No, it's not that, my liege, it's just that I was thinking about it and I have something better to say rather than what I've written'.

They didn't say anything else. They just shifted their paperwork and glared at me for too long. I decided to play on through, like rubbing a magic sponge on an injury and walking it off down the pitch.

'I love this campus' I began. 'Before I came here I knew very little of the world outside of Lancashire but being down south has shown me things. The friends I have made here are friends for life. They are the kind of people I would swear by, the kind of people who would jump in front of a sniper for me. We have a bond, a brotherhood, it is the kind of understanding and friendship it is impossible to describe and yet here I am, being asked to do just that. The important thing about campus is it is one of the few places in the world where people care about each other. There is a real sense of community here and I love that. This isn't just university for us, this is our life. For three years-'.

'I'm sorry to interrupt you Mr. Sutcliffe but-'.

'Alright, I've been here for four but-'.

'That's not the-'.

'No! You listen!' I bellowed, and then blinked back the tears that came up in my eyes because I loved my life so much and not because I'm a fucking girl. 'You told me to write this and I did, so you're going to listen. This isn't just about education. I'm learning a lot more outside of the classroom than I am in it, and don't start saying that isn't the point of being here and I should be going to all of my lectures because I go to some, most, more than some people who I won't name, like Jay Balzik. What I mean is you can only study a few hours a day but you can learn for up to twenty-four hours a day, if you aren't sleeping, or eating, or playing football, so I'm learning now, and I think you should take that into consideration before you start getting carried away and calling people up to explain themselves like this. I think I should stay on campus for these reasons and you can't kick me out because I'll be straight on the phone to the authorities'.

I stopped and adjusted my tie from where it had fallen outside of my suit jacket in the fury with which I had delivered my speech. I felt pleased with myself though. It was in the back of the net and I was running back into my own half with my shirt pulled over my head.

I let out a deep breath I hadn't even realised I had held the whole time and a bead of sweat slid past my heavy eyebrow and made me wince a bit.

'Thank you very much for that colourful performance Mr. Sutcliffe, I don't think any of us could say it was exactly what was expected but you never fail to fall outside of the agreed parameters'. I took that as the compliment it had been intended as. 'We have actually concluded we will grant you one last chance to show us what you are made of, as it were. I don't want to have to gather my esteemed colleagues together in this manner again, especially on such a beautiful day. Now, back to your studies'.

I walked out in total disbelief. I had actually done it. It was without a doubt my most successful assignment to date. That would have been a First grade in itself. I took the sweeping staircase of the Manor House which held the meeting rooms and administration offices two steps at a time and swung the fat front door open wide. I was out in the sunshine. I grabbed my mobile phone from my sticky hot pocket and rung up Dad, thinking he would be really pleased with how I had done. I was slightly annoyed they hadn't recorded the interview because I would loved to have watched the whole thing back with my old man, so he could see how well I had done, maybe with bits in slow-motion like they do on *Match of the Day*. It had barely rung before he answered.

'Sutcliffe Janitorial Services'.

'Dad, it's me' I said.

'You're welcome' he replied.

'No... what?'

'You're still on that shitty campus right?'

'Yeah but...'

'Well you're welcome'. A car came steaming past the roundabout outside the Manor House. I pressed the phone to my ear and stepped up onto the grass edge to get out of it's path.

'What do you mean Dad?'

'Let's just say your old man had to sort matters out again, so, you're welcome'.

'What do you mean?'

'Made a bit of a donation so they felt obliged to keep you onboard'.

'How much?'

'Let's just say it is your inheritance'. I couldn't believe what I was hearing.

'What?'

'You're deaf now as well as dumb are you, I said, it is your inheritance'.

'No but Dad I…'

'I expect a return on my investment son. If you don't come back here with a degree then you don't come back. You can spend your days down in London with your poncey little southern mates. You get me?'

'Yeah, but Dad, I…'

The phone disconnected. He had hung up on me. I was bloody fuming. I could have handled it myself. I had them all on the ropes and was giving them the once over, it was down to that. The money didn't even matter, it had been me. I had sorted it out. I headed to the bar.

I couldn't believe my eyes when I got there. There were none of the usual lot about, none of my boys. There were just a couple of foreign students stressing over some report they were obviously due to hand in, and then Oliver and his lot.

They were alright but you couldn't really sit and banter with them about football because eventually they got into other conversations, about stuff I didn't understand, especially his skinny mate with the curly hair. He didn't even like football. You can't trust a boy who doesn't like football, it's like a bird that can't fly, they're probably all faggots or something.

I stepped up to the bar.

'Alright Pete, where is everyone?'

The barman shrugged back at me. He was a man of few words.

'I'll have a Stella' I said. I figured eventually they would come in, or someone would, someone I could talk to. I could just sit tight and wait for them.

'Pete, can I borrow the paper?' I asked, pointing to a copy of *The Sun* flipped in half on the bar. He mumbled something in response and shuffled off to hide. I grabbed the paper and found a table as far from them as possible, I didn't want to have to hear any of their bollocks as I got lost in the news.

I sat down and turned to the back pages, where the football is, because that's all a newspaper is good for anyway. The ten pages in from the back page, that's the interesting bit. The rest is boring.

I wasn't far enough from them as it turned out. I could still hear them and they were being idiots, jabbering on about things I didn't understand. That was the problem with law students, they were just hassle because they could use all these words that nobody else had heard of, all Latin and that. I would have got more sense out of the foreign kids in the corner. There was no point in entering an argument with them because they didn't fight fair.

I wanted to still rile them up though, to show them for interrupting me from looking at the pictures in the back of the newspaper, and the only thing for it was to blast them with some old school garage tunes. I knew they were all a bunch of greebos and it would piss them off, and maybe drive them up and out of my bar. It was something I had accidentally seen in a documentary on hostage situations where they blast shit music and the terrorists give up because they can't take it anymore.

I put a couple of quid in the jukebox and selected as much of the *Pure Garage 2004* album as I could.

Yeah I really liked it, it was wicked, wicked, wicked!

They all turned to see where the noise was coming from. I thought I was winning, but then Oliver yelled over the top of it at Pete, who was pouring himself another pint.

'Oi Pete, turn this shit down, I can't fucking think'.

I could just make out his words over the harsh tasty beats. The music suddenly cut out.

'But Pete,' I cried, 'I already put two quid in'.

'You can have it on quietly' he said, like he was my fucking dad. I then had to sit listening to the whispered sounds of DJ Luck and MC Neat for twenty minutes while they rabbited on about a bunch of nonsense, I couldn't even focus on the sport. Eventually I downed my pint and left.

That night was the Beach Party at the bar. I had really been looking forward to it because I had managed to get one of those red floats like they have on Baywatch. It made me look like a young Hasselhoff. Some of the lads were just heading down to the bar in shorts while the chunkier and more self-conscious boys were wearing a t-shirt over the top of the uniform red shorts. I was wearing a t-shirt but only because it said 'Lifeguard' on it and I didn't get much chance to wear it beyond that one night a year.

We arrived at about ten o'clock. There were at least twenty of us, all in uniform and it was such a laugh. We had started out the night with a game of 'Down it' where at any point you could shout 'down it!' at someone and they had to down their pint.

It's brilliant and you get wankered and almost anyone can play because there's only one rule, which is down it.

The night carried on in the usual style. Pingu the DJ played all the hits. We did all the synchronised dances; *Soulja Boy* and *Cha-Cha Slide*. We showed everyone we were the kings of campus. I saw the boys who had been in the bar earlier that day sniggering to themselves like they knew better than the football lads. That was the problem with law students, they always thought they knew better than the football lads, and they obviously didn't.

As soon as the Baywatch theme song came on we showed them though. I watched them all scarper rather than reveal their puny bodies. The thing with the Baywatch theme was as soon as it played all the lads took their t-shirts or vests off and started swinging them around their heads and singing along. On the other hand those law boys were all talk and when it came down to it we had all the moves and that's it at the end of the day, that's what matters, because actions speak louder than talking does.

One of the girls started giving me the eye as I was dancing about on the stage to a remix of the *A-Team* theme. I swaggered over to her and offered her a drink, because when it comes to the birds I know you have to be a gentleman. For some reason this seemed to gain the attention of the other lads who were all elbowing and whispering to each other as we queued at the bar.

I talked to her about things she liked because a gentleman has to ask questions and be attentive. One of the major advantages of being such a player on campus was I could get served before the majority of the other wankers. I snapped my fingers at the pretty little blonde barmaid as she walked past but obviously the tunes were too loud for her to hear it. I took out a ten-pound note and waved it across the bar to get her attention. I turned back to the girl I was with.

'What do you want to drink?' I shouted in her ear.

'Double Amaretto and coke please'.

Lucky I had a tenner out, I thought to myself.

Eventually I got served and after struggling to talk any further she suggested we step out into the darkened foyer to chat.

'What's your name' I asked, grabbing her hand as we smashed through the double doors out of the bar and into the quiet.

'Camilla' she said.

'What a beautiful name'.

'Thank you'.

'And what do you study Camilla?'

I had learnt how to talk to women by watching the way Cilla asked questions on Blind Date. It was pretty simple. You just took what they said and thought of another thing to ask them that wasn't in their answer.

'Nursing' she said.

'And do you like nursing?'

'Yeah, it's alright. What about you?' she asked, chewing on her straw all sexy like.

'I'm in business' I said, which I had learnt sounded better than saying I was repeating Business Studies.

'Oh wow, so you're like a business man'.

'Yeah, essentially' I said. 'Do you want to go and dance, it's just that they're playing a song I really like'.

It was one of the old school garage classics that had been on the jukebox earlier. One I hadn't been able to enjoy because Pete had been made to turn it down.

'Yeah, that would be nice'.

About twenty minutes later things were getting a bit tasty on the dance floor. We were like Johnny and Baby and I had my hand tucked round her as she stood facing away from me with her booty shaking up and down my muscly thigh. I felt like such a pimp. All the lads were watching and I thought to myself, this is going to be a good night Iggy. She was well up for it and she could feel through my shorts that I was too.

In the end I had to fold it up and tuck it into the elastic at the top because it was starting to hurt. I did it really discreetly though and then carried on dancing, one hand raised in the air, pointing at each of my boys and making a face that said *that's right, I'm all over this like a pro, so stand back and watch because this is just what I do*. I was a pro and everyone had to know about it. They still thought it was funny and were egging me on and stuff.

In the end I decided enough was enough and posed the question.

'Camilla, do you fancy coming back to mine so I can satisfy you in every way possible?'

She turned around and looked at me. The bass kept on thumping and the lights kept on flashing against her face and then she narrowed her eyes and nodded. That's consent right there, that's consent.

She then grabbed me by the back of my hair and pulled me down to her mouth. I kissed her and let my tongue explore all around her mouth and then she put her tongue out and we were just a pair of tongues slapping together on a dance floor. It was magic.

Moments later she grabbed me and led me outside.

'I can't wait' she said to me, and I realised by the way the elastic was cutting into me I couldn't either. Jay and Marco were working on the door and they said goodbye to us as we headed off into the night.

When I looked back Jay gave me a sly wink and Marco was miming a shagging motion. I stuck my tongue out and let Camilla lead me to the bushes opposite the security office.

It was dead romantic out because there was all this moonlight pouring down on the campus, and it wasn't too cloudy so there were stars out and we were like Aladdin and Jasmine in a whole new world, with a new fantastic point of view.

Then I grabbed her arse under her skirt and she let out a sigh and reached up to kiss me again. We were just on the edge of the bushes and she was drunkenly leaning back into them, so eventually we fell together and I was on top of her in the hedgerow and it had that nice smell like the campus does every other Tuesday when they come round and cut the grass. She rolled me off of her and slowly pulled on the white drawstring of my shorts. This loosened them off just enough that I was able to tug them down and reveal what I had been hiding for far too long.

Just then she got this funny look on her face, like how people look when they've been out drinking, and they're having fun and then all of a sudden they realise they have had too many shots and they're going to vomit.

She sort of bolted upright and she let go of me, and then before I could sit up, or pull my shorts back up she was gone, and she was running, and in the quiet of the night, with the distant sound of DJ Pingu playing some class tunes I could hear her crying and stumbling, making her way back towards the entrance of the bar and towards Jay and Marco.

I got up and started running after her to try and work out what was going on. My head was swimming, and it was only partly down to the beers. I couldn't work it out, moments before she had been gagging for it and then she was running from me. The girl was gone in the head.

****

'And that's your story is it?' asked PC Walton, edging his way around the back of me so I couldn't make eye contact with him like I had always been taught to so people would believe what you say.

'Yeah, I'm telling you she wanted it. She led me on and then I dunno, got freaked out or whatever, I never did anything. I never forced her!'

PC Walton appeared back round the front of me and pressed pause on the tape machine.

'You're lucky you've got mates who are willing to lie for you, you fucking scumbag, but I will get you. One more slip up matey boy and you won't know you're alive until you hear the clunk of them bars shutting behind you'.

He pressed record again.

'I have here the testimony of Mr. Jay Balzik who says he saw you and Miss Camilla Buckhall head off together into the night. He says although you had both been drinking neither of you seemed intoxicated to the point you were not aware of yourselves. You're free to go Mr. Sutcliffe. We have no further questions'.

I couldn't believe it, the boys had come through for me. Justice had been served.

The thing was something like that doesn't go away like it should. It gets sensationalised and people don't remember the ending. As far as campus was concerned from that point on I was a nonce or something. I had to try and write it all down to explain it to someone. I hope it makes sense and I hope you believe me.

The Night Of The Fridge Graveyard

MICHAEL
March 2007

There was nothing but the empty echo of my footsteps as I stumbled up the stairs, across the shared landing of the flat, and into the room I hadn't bothered to lock because I simply had no idea I would be away from it for so long. My intention had been to rush down to the shop in order to get some dinner before they closed up for the night. Instead I had been dragged into a bout of drinking which only ended when the shutters on the bar were pulled down upon us.

It hadn't even been the regular hooligans I spent so much of my time with that had managed to coax out the drinker in me. Instead it was the cool indie sect who intimidated me ever so softly, who seemed so far beyond my capabilities as a music fan. They wore t-shirts promoting bands I hadn't got into. I couldn't help but feel underdeveloped as a person when I was around them, but it wasn't as a result of their spite, in fact it was in no way intentional. They just operated on a higher plain, and I found them absolutely fascinating.

I dashed back and forth over my cell of a room searching for something to wear which they would approve of. I don't know why it bothered me so much. I wanted something cutting edge enough for them because everything was a copy of a copy of a copy (as *Fight Club* had taught me). They had promised a share in the case of beers they had secured at the flat they all seemed to occupy if I hurried. I don't know how they always seemed to be in the same flat, alongside other comers and goers. I knew there could only have been five bedrooms and yet there were at least six of them.

I was already wearing my skinniest jeans, procured from a girlfriend with whom the relationship had long since expired. I decided I needed something cool and vintage to pair it with on top. On the back of my chair lay the *Dark Side Of The Moon* t-shirt I wasn't overly keen on because of the focus on the rainbow on the reverse of it. I associated rainbows with the gay pride movement.

I decided it could be considered edgy to wear it, so pulled it over my lithe frame. I threw my zip through black jacket under my arm and started out again. I had a date with the night.

I was wary of taking too much time to get ready, it was possible to fall out of the loop with them within fifteen minutes. I suppose a part of the draw was the fact they seemed to be doing much more interesting courses than the stodgy pulp of Law I was reading. They were in Events Management or Film & Television Production. They were creative and wild.

By the time I got to the flat the party had already established an order. They had all got back and settled in for the night. Caera and Bark were sat knee to knee with just an acoustic guitar between them as they tried to establish a chord progress in their collective mind. Teagan and Layla were in the corner giggling to themselves and chewing on straws dipped into bottles of blue alcopops. Ryan was busily spinning the central wheel of an iPod connected to a massive pair of speakers balanced precariously on the windowsill. Kennedy was laying face down on a closed up ironing board. I had *arrived*. This was the campus's very own Warhol's Factory. The walls were covered in splashes of dirt, finger paints, silver foil and posters stolen from the bar and from magazines. The floor was littered with takeaway wrappers, newspapers, bottle caps and drug paraphernalia. The air was thick with smoke and I had no choice but to join in. The problem then was I didn't want to disturb them. They all looked so happy, as though they knew what they were doing, were set in their ways, and I was about to interrupt it all. I felt like a child pulling a dollhouse over so the contents fell crashing to the floor.

I lit a cigarette and leant against the doorway like I had entered a Wild West saloon. Ryan turned from the window and was the first to speak.

'Michael, come in. Do you want a beer?'

Everyone else turned to celebrate my arrival and invite me in. Before I could give Ryan an answer, or even exhale the smoke I was holding in he had carefully placed the iPod on the narrow windowsill, plucked a *Biere Speciale* from the open crate on the table and was holding it out to me.

'Have you got a bottle opener?' I asked, putting my hand out to meet his own, and accepting the beer. Ryan scanned the immediate area, the dirty table and the gritty floor and shrugged. He pulled the bottle back from me and jammed the top into his mouth, yanking the cap off with his teeth in one smooth movement. He spat it to the floor, where it bounced and caught amongst the rubbish. He passed the beer back to me with a grin.

'My dentist said I have to stop doing that' he said.

'Doesn't surprise me'.

'It's just easier than finding an opener in here'.

Ryan pulled back a chair and indicated for me to sit down before pulling one up for himself. We sat awkwardly for a moment, watching Caera and Bark play the intro to a song I didn't recognise at the time. As if it had emerged from thin air Caera had a single octave xylophone in her lap and was playing along to Bark's acoustic guitar. It would be three years before I found out it was a Coconut Records song, *West Coast*. That's how far ahead they were from me in musical tastes.

Between attempts or takes of the track they would take a moment to drag on cigarettes otherwise sat idly balanced on the edge of the crammed ashtray. They would then tousle their hair before trying the same song over again. I turned my attention to Kennedy who was still on the ironing board but appeared to be talking softly to it, and caressing it, one thin spidery leg in purple leggings snaking up the side. His over-straightened hair hung lank over most of his face.

'Is he alright?' I asked.

I had a strange relationship with Kennedy. I think we had both had a go on the same girl in the not too recent past, which was the kind of silent bond a lot of the boys on campus shared. At the same time I was fairly sure he had no idea who I was. He was one of those people who took far too many drugs, to the point his personality was mute. He was just 'druggie'. I know I am partial to the sporadic joint, pill, bomb or line but this was something else. I had seen the guy huffing glue in a bag. I didn't even know that was a real thing people did, or was even possible to do. I thought it was a horror story told by teachers and parents when you're little to keep you safe and boring, like the perils of quicksand.

I had also seen him drink poppers.

'What's he on tonight?' I asked.

'Ket'.

'What's that?'

'Ketamine'.

'Oh'.

In my own naïve and trivial drug habit I had not come across Ketamine until this point. It is best known as an anaesthetic for veterinary purposes, most commonly as a horse tranquiliser but of course the hideous youth had decided to start using it for recreational purposes and an entire counterculture had begun. Years later, when dating a vet, I attempted to get her to sell some to me for my own experimentation. She rightfully declined.

Ketamine use, or abuse, was what I watched the effects of that evening. Kennedy was coming down, he was over the hump of it. As far as I know he had spent the evening in on his own, while everyone else was at the bar and he had chosen to indulge himself. They had found him on the ironing board upon their return to the flat and he was yet to move. He wasn't capable or aware, but he was shifting, in the same way a baby will move before it works out how to crawl.

'He's like an advert for the dangers of drugs' said Ryan. I snapped back into focus. I had been watching Kennedy so closely, analysing his position and breathing and spasm-like movements like a proud parent, leaning over to watch him convulse and gurgle. My cigarette was down to the nub, and the ash had long since dropped to the floor to join the other mess. I sipped from my beer and Caera gave up on the xylophone.

'You're a musician' she said to me, 'play something'. She pushed the instrument across the table to me and then threw the thin plastic mallets down on the keys. She looked at me expectantly, her pretty green Irish eyes and baby face smiling.

For anyone to call me a musician is laughable, especially myself. I play guitar, and can just about hammer a few chords on the piano but it is a far stretch from being confident whenever an instrument gets shoved across a table at me.

'You should wear this as you play' Caera added. She picked up a red hard hat with 'Thirst Aid' written along the front. Someone had scrawled an '*s*' in marker pen after the white writing. Attached to the hat were two drinks holders with a thick plastic straw connecting them and dangling from the front.

Caera stood, reached across the table, and put the hat over the top of my unruly curls as though she were crowning me. It felt tight and unbalanced.

'Fill him up Ry' she said.

Ryan and I both chose to ignore the innuendo, but we both blushed. It was down to our mutual awkward nature. Ryan duly removed the lids from two more bottles of beer with his teeth and placed them in the hat as I tried to balance it.

'Now play, and drink' said Caera. I felt like the village idiot, but it is sometimes a role I will assume entirely of my own volition so I did exactly as I was told.

As I began to suck on the straw my mouth filled with foam rather than beer. I can safely say there is a reason Thirst Aid hats are retained mostly for comedic purposes. They are not particularly effective as a means of drinking.

I managed to hit a couple of keys before the foam swilling in my mouth became overbearing and I had to stop before I exploded. I tried to swallow as much down as possible, for fear of dribbling in front of the girls. For a second there was an immediate fear the drink would pour from my nose. As I pushed the sensation back, along with the tears from my eyes it slowly became easier and before I knew it I had drained both bottles. Ryan, Bark and Caera cheered. I looked up at them with weeping bloodshot eyes and took the hat off. I wiped my mouth with the back of my hand and tried to look pleased with myself, and assure myself I hadn't just been invited to be the court jester for the group.

Should I be proud of myself? I wondered.

The sudden rowdiness had brought Kennedy into a state of almost consciousness. He was *really* enjoying the ironing board. I don't know what the hallucinations Ketamine induces are like but it looked pretty impressive from where I stood. All of his movements seemed to stem from his hips, and as he gyrated around on the floor like Tom Jones we couldn't help but laugh.

'It's not funny!' screamed Teagan, causing our laughter to be cut completely. It is safe to say she was the only girl in the room I couldn't have been coaxed into bed by, and that is saying quite a lot. 'He could be dying' she added, putting her empty bottle down and getting down on her hands and knees to inspect him for signs of life. I cannot remember if she was a nursing student but she certainly came across like one.

What she didn't seem to understand was that Kennedy was like tinned food or the cockroach. There was nothing that was going to destroy him, his shelf life was forever.

Somehow the raucous laughter being made at his expense broke through and he suddenly bolted to his feet. It struck us all as being the most unusual thing to happen. We dropped into silence once more. He stood hunched over his ironing board lover for a second, holding himself like he was on death row. We were all completely still. He could either have been a cobra ready to strike or a mouse ready to dive back into the hole. We couldn't be sure.

Six pairs of eyes followed as he walked between us and out into the hall. We quickly got up as a collective and headed out to watch what he was going to do. It was only then I noticed what Kennedy was wearing.

It was not only the purple leggings which made up his unusual ensemble but also a white t-shirt so short it didn't meet his protruding hipbones and a number of necklaces and bangles, which fascinated him as he walked. He was like the Mr T of being fucked. We followed him down the narrow corridor step for step. His hands were drawn up to his chest, and he raised his legs higher than was necessary for the practice of walking. I was instantly reminded of the velociraptors that mess up the kitchen in Jurassic Park.

'Where's he going?' I asked to anyone who might have known.

'Shhh' came the response in stereo.

Kennedy opened the door and started out into the darkness of the night, towards the road that circled the block of flats. He was suddenly illuminated by the lamppost that hung over the corner. For a second I thought he was about to be abducted.

As soon as his feet hit the tarmac his balance seemed to go completely. He walked like a child coursing through the incoming tide. It seemed to take an incredibly concerted effort to free his foot from the ground for each step. He would then swinging the raised leg in a great arc and slap it down on the floor. He would then repeat the same gesture for the other half of his body. He was on a sinking ship of hallucination and we were all completely hooked.

'Do you think he's going to see what's-her-name' Ryan eventually asked when the echo of his footsteps was starting to sink away.

'Yeah, I assume that's his intention' said Bark.

'Will he be alright?' I asked, genuinely worried he could get hit by a car or worse still, come back.

'Oh I've seen him in worse states' said Caera, and she ducked back inside to get another beer.

Once Kennedy was out of sight he became very much out of mind. Rather than returning to the kitchen we decided to camp down in the hall which meant we lost all concept of time. There were no windows in the hall and the overhead strip lighting made it seem like we were in a constant state of midday. Despite the mild ache coming in behind my eyes, urging me to give up, to call it a night and head off to bed I pushed on. I was having fun and it felt like the night wasn't over yet. There was still more to be had of it. I sat nursing one of the last of the beers as Ryan told me of his plans for the future, after we had graduated.

'I would like to see the world' he said.

I nodded along. I wanted to see the world too, but we were all more than aware of the cost involved, and the amount of debt we were already in. It would take a lot of effort and hard work before we could turn the little minus sign next to our bank balance into a plus.

'Where would you like to go?' I asked him.

'There are loads of places. I would like to live in New York at some point, I'd love to do that actually'.

'You would need something waiting for you though. You couldn't just fly over there and assume it would work out' I replied, trying to play the role of realist and ground him.

'Well yeah, at first but you could just go with it. The joy of a degree is it's going to be recognised anywhere, and the further away you are the less likely they will have heard of this campus and therefore won't be aware of the reputation it holds. You could pretend you were basically aristocracy'.

I laughed.

'You think that could work?'

'Yeah, why not?' he asked, and I couldn't give him an answer. 'Where would you like to go?'

It was something I had thought about for a long time. In an ideal world there are any number of places I would like to go and I thought of those instead of the limited places available as possibilities. I spread my arms to give myself room to answer.

'I would like to travel across America' I said.

'Oh cool, yeah. I had a friend who did that'.

Of course he did. They all had friends who had done anything I had thought of, and had done it much better than I could, and in a much more unique and cool way than I thought imaginable. I knew it wasn't an original idea of mine though.

'I would like to go from Massachusetts to San Francisco' I concluded, settling on a starting point and destination.

'Like Kerouac?'

'Yeah, like Kerouac'.

I took another sip from my beer.

'Hey, were you here the night we went to the fridge graveyard?'

I tried to work out how drunk I was, and whether there was a reason the two words sounded so odd alongside one another.

'The *where*?' I asked.

'The fridge graveyard'

'What is the fridge graveyard?'

'Oh, it's this really cool place we found by accident, we'll take you'.

Before I could argue, or even reason it through, Ryan had announced the plan to take me to the fridge graveyard. I couldn't be sure what it meant because I wasn't with the kind of people who spoke straight. There was always a sarcastic sheen to their comments. Things had silly nicknames. I didn't think what I would find would be what I imagined when I thought of the pairing of those two words. They refused to tell me any more of the details, and simply repeated Ryan's platitude that it was a cool spot in the woods. They said I would love it. I had been made the same promise before enough times I simply didn't believe it.

Pushing any images of the Manson family murders out of my head I picked my jacket up from where it had fallen to the floor. Everyone loaded up with whatever they felt they would need for the trek and we headed for the front door together.

As we squeezed our way outside I realised the night was slowly giving way to the grizzly grey of morning. I tried to remember what day it had been when I had headed out to get dinner, and therefore what day it was becoming. I wondered if I would collapse if I didn't get some food in me.

Then it hit me, it was a Monday. I had lectures at nine. It was getting on for four. I knew if I went to bed there was no way I would make it to my class. There was no way I could operate on just the four hours of sleep available between the moment of sudden realisation and when I would need to get up. There was only one plausible solution, or so I thought in the moment. I would have to stay up, go straight to my lecture, and then sleep afterwards. I had a free afternoon and could just sleep it off. It seemed like the most sensible thing, to just keep going, to ride through on the adrenaline and possibly a caffeine boost, and just deal with sleep later. Sleep could wait.

We headed off the road and round the back of the collection of industrial-sized bins where everyone was supposed to drag their black sacks of household waste to.

Usual protocol however was to leave them outside the flat's front door with the intention of taking them to the bins on route to the bar or a lesson, and then completely forgetting about it. Overnight they became victims of the badgers and foxes that strolled about in the surrounding woodland of the campus. You would head out in a rush for a lecture to find the plastic remains of your microwavable tikka masala spread across the path.

For the three years I was at university I was genuinely scared of the woodland creatures that occupied the campus of an evening. They were said to have attacked people. I'm possibly not bullshitting when I say a girl got her leg broken by a badger.

From the bins we headed through a gap in the trees and along a path I had either never spotted before or had simply never been concerned enough by to follow. Eventually it was hard to believe we were still on campus grounds.

'Guys, are we still on campus grounds?' I said.

'Not sure' called Caera over her shoulder from where she was leading the way with Bark.

'It must be' said Ryan, almost trying to reassure me we weren't about to get set upon by farmers, or worse still, in trouble with campus security. We strolled through woodland like the boys in Stand By Me, telling stories and taking the piss out of each other. I half expected to be jumped by a young Keifer Sutherland. Unfortunately it didn't happen.

The further we walked the more daylight seemed to chase us down. I was worried what could be revealed in the light of day. Operating as two different people often had that effect upon me.

Eventually we came alongside a barbed wire fence. Beyond it was a sloped field ascending before us.

'It isn't much further now' whispered Ryan, as we seemed to have drifted into silent running mode. There was nothing to listen to but the sounds of our feet through the dry undergrowth, and the calls overhead of the birds I couldn't name. I kept trudging on, following the drooping heads of those in front of me. The path opened up and I saw the fridge graveyard.

In some ways I wish there was some kind of incredible description I could give but it was what it was. In front of me were around thirty fridges, mostly upright but a few were on their sides or backs, either as a result of student pranksters or heavy winds. They were dabbled in leaves and had pools of water collected in their dented surfaces. They served no purpose but to show how disposable everything eventually becomes.

There was a time when each of those white goods held dominion over a kitchen, when students would stand in it's cold light, staring at the shelves, hoping inspiration or a meal would appear upon the empty bars. They had cooled countless crates of beer and their bottom drawers had been host to every kind of vegetable, purchased with good intentions but left uneaten to turn to pulp and grey sludge.

There was an eerie silence over it, like someone had just walked in on an examination in progress. The fridges were the kitchen equivalent of a wedding dress hung in the window of a charity shop.

'It's cool, right?' said Ryan, breaking the silence over me as if it were a magic spell to be lifted.

'Yeah, I've never seen anything like it. How did you find this?'

'I can't remember, it must have been by accident. I like it though. It makes you realise how quick we are to throw things away'.

Ryan gazed off into the middle distance. At first I thought he had spotted something, but he was just being reflective and sad.

He was right of course, I had never felt as wasteful as I did as a student. Not only would I end up throwing away food that was long past it's sell by date simply because I hadn't bothered to eat it, but I had also wasted an awful lot of time. It wasn't just my time either, it was everyone else's.

The whole thing served as some kind of hideous allegory. I was in the fridge graveyard for a reason, I was a disposed fridge. All I wanted to do was pull my feet up and start running. In my head I could see it clearly. Without breaking pace I would run all the way back through the woods, back onto campus, up the road, past the library and over to my flat. I didn't know what I would do then but it felt important.

I suddenly took stock of what I was thinking and concluded it was just the late night/early morning status of my brain slipping away and leaving me a little vacuous.

'Layla, climb in one' said Bark, and we all grabbed her limbs and helped her in. As soon as the door was shut someone tipped it over and all we could make out were her muffled screams from inside. It took about ten seconds of our laughter catching in the silence of the morning before anyone was able to get a grip on the door.

Opening it up again we saw why she had been screaming. The water that had been gathered in the door and hollow side panels of the fridge had flushed into the chamber where she was laying as it was tipped over.

It was like a magic trick, where we had put in a beautiful, if not somewhat wasted and spaced out assistant, and what had emerged was a half-drowned and fully pissed off rat.

'I'm fucking soaked' she said, which seemed odd because I didn't imagine her to be the swearing type. I tried to avoid staring at her soaked chest by feigning interest in the selection of trees which overhung the area. I made no efforts to help. Bark did the honourable thing and took off his hoodie to protect her from the crisp morning air.

She snatched the jumper and wrapped it around herself, swearing some more. Caera took a run up and kicked one of the upright fridges over onto its side, where it splattered up mud and mulch. We all laughed again at her recklessness and began our slow walk back to campus.

As we were coming up to the open field in the light of a Monday, Bark turned to me.

'Have you ever been cow tipping?' he asked.

'What's cow tipping?'

'Well cows sleep standing up-'.

'Yeah'.

'So you run over-'.

'Yeah?'

'And tip them over'.

'Oh' I said with a stop.

'Yeah, what were you expecting?'

'Well I guess that' I concluded.

'Michael, everything we do is what it is. There's not some great secret to the way we carry anything out. We are just as confused and lost as everyone else. What did you think the fridge graveyard was going to be?'

I shrugged.

'Come on' Bark said, and held the barbed wire up so I could pass through unscathed. Once everyone else was through Bark ducked under the wire, keeping it free from himself with one hand as he swung his bulk through. We then faced a hill, which led up to another section of woods on the far side. Just before the entrance to the woods I could make out a number of cows stood about, peaceful and perfectly still from our vantage point.

'Is this private land?' I asked. Nobody seemed to know, or at least they didn't tell me one way or the other. They just started trekking up the hill towards the black and white subjects of our intended vandalism. Once again I joined the troops.

We were halfway across the field before anyone looked up again.

'Shit, they're already up!' someone said.

'What?!' someone else replied.

'The cows are already awake!'

Everything took on a blur, like watching video camera footage of someone on the run. The cows had the upper ground and were coming right for us. It was the Light Brigade but we were running back, refusing to follow orders, and trying to work out whether we could jump the barbed wire between ourselves and the relative safety of the woodland.

In the moment it sounded as if the charging hooves were surrounding us, as though they had the pack mentality of velociraptors, like they were all just Kennedy, cloned and in costume. We scurried through the fence, catching sleeves and laces on the spikes of coiled wire. The air was full of raised voices and curse words.

By the time we caught our collective breath and looked back there wasn't a sign of the pursuers we had assumed were just a hooves-length behind us. They appeared to have lost interest in our blood and returned to their cud.

We started laughing and didn't stop until we were safe, back on the edge of campus and as much civilisation as we were used to. There was an instant relief as we peeled back the last of the leaves and caught sight of the blocks of flats beyond the bins. It felt like we had been somewhere, seen something, learnt some kind of lesson. My brain was too fried to completely grasp exactly what it could have been but I was aware of an enlightenment on the tip of my tongue.

'What do we do now?' asked Caera, as we sauntered through the abandoned road of our makeshift student town. She started kicking a bin, which was screwed to a lamppost on a hinge. She always seemed to be kicking things. I put it down to unresolved anger issues.

Bark picked up the green shell of another bin and put it over his head, running around in circles and then chasing Teagan. I don't know in hindsight why there were so many bins around all the time. On another occasion I can remember using the shell of one as a sled in winter.

What kind of *Stig of the Dump* education was I getting?

Dave, a member of Campus Security, who was more than used to our antics, chose this moment to walk round the corner, trying to work out why there were students out of their beds. It wasn't like there was anything against the rules about us being out at four or five in the morning but when your after hour activities include smashing up fridges, getting chased by cows and kicking campus property they tend to draw a line. All of a sudden our silliness came to a complete standstill. It was like we were at a boarding school and had been caught reading comics after lights out.

'What's going on guys?' asked Dave.

'Nothing Dave' said Bark through his plastic cover.

'Do you think you could take that bin off your head?'

'Yeah sure Dave, no problem'.

Bark lifted the bin up over his head, and dropped it to the floor where it bounced and rolled to a stop by the hedges.

'Do you think you should put it back where it came from?' Dave asked.

'Do you think I should put it back where it came from?'

'Yes Bark, I do'.

It was interesting Dave was on first name terms with us all. It showed amongst the thousand or so students on campus our actions had called us to the attention of the security team on enough occasions they had taken the time to learn our individual names.

'Michael, what are you doing with these guys?' Dave asked me.

I don't really feel like explaining how Dave knew who I was. It wasn't for the same reason he knew Caera or Ryan or Bark. It was a separate incident and nearly got me and my closest friends kicked off campus. I had been attempting to keep my nose clean since.

'We are friends' I declared.

'Where's Oliver?' asked Dave.

'I dunno, in bed, with his girlfriend probably'.

'Oh I see' said Dave, presuming I had been abandoned for a girl. 'Just stop kicking shit about'. He started walking back to his post. We all yelled our apologies after him.

It felt as though the interaction had well and truly put our tails between our legs. It had taken the air out of what we were doing. Finally we were hit with the cold light of day and nobody liked it. All it meant was we had spent another evening of nothing in particular, and it had come to an end. It all felt like a terrible anti-climax, like the end of a French film. There was no real resolution, just a confused audience sat with clenched brows staring at the rolling credits.

As far as I was concerned it brought on the harsh realisation there was no way I was going to be in any fit state to head to lectures. I had been awake for twenty-one hours, and had been drinking fairly solidly for nine of those. I couldn't work out when I had last eaten anything. I stunk of cheap beer and cigarettes and my eyes were like fresh bullet wounds. I was completely at the end of my tether. The wall suddenly hit me, the point a marathon runner has to break through. I couldn't do it though. I hadn't spent months in training. I didn't have the right shoes on.

Within seconds I was walking back to my flat with my hands shoved deep in my pockets to ward off the cold. Within minutes I had my head buried into my pillow and unconsciousness.

Madcat On The Prowl

LUCAS
November 2007

The whole thing started because I changed course. That's how I ended up in a situation so stupid I had to call home and report it, because it was just a bit bizarre and I needed to reality check and ensure it wasn't just me that found it strange. That's the problem with spending so long on campus, away from family and friends and the things that make up life. Your visions get a little bit tweaked and you're never really sure how you are supposed to react to anything. It's all just a little surreal sometimes.

I had decided I shouldn't have been focusing on business as a straight subject, and that I would be better suited to Telecommunications. It seemed to combine the aspects of business I enjoyed with the opportunity to work from anywhere in the world. As I said, that's where the problems started.

Studying Telecommunications meant I didn't get to spend any time with the friends I had made in my previous class. It meant I was a little fish in a sea of operator sharks, people who it turned out were not from the UK. I have to be very careful in my descriptions because it could come across as being racist but I promise that is not my intention at all. I don't have a bigoted bone in my body. It was just an unusual experience for me, something different entirely to walk into a classroom and be the only white boy in there. I guess it must be how the only black boy in my business class felt. I had never really thought about it in those terms though, which is just further evidence I don't judge people based on the colour of their skin. It's not an issue at all, it's just different. This is a story of cultural differences, and miscommunications and is therefore worth mentioning.

It makes sense a lot of the students studying Telecommunications were from overseas, I heard my dad complaining about Indian call centres all the time.

I had managed to coast through the first month of lectures without having anything to do with anyone else on my course. When the situation called for it I would apologise to someone if they accidentally sat on my hand, or I would lend out or borrow a biro but that was as far as it went. We had our time together in the classroom and then I would go off to meet my friends at our flat, or in the bar, and they would go off to do their thing. That was until a Thursday afternoon in November when I was blocked from leaving by the boy who had been sitting beside me that day.

I have always been terrible with names, and the problem was made all the more difficult for me by the fact I was a simple boy from just outside Milton Keynes who had never known anyone with anything even edging close to being an unusual name. Yet changing course meant I found myself in a room with fifty unusual names.

By this point I had twigged a few but due to my habit of daydreaming I had changed them, playing about with them in my head, and turning them into characters based on how the strange sounds went together, or how they looked. That was why the boy who approached me will from hereon in only be known by the name I gave him because I was too ignorant to learn it properly; Madcat.

Madcat was slightly shorter than me, and slightly hunched, owing mostly to the immense layers of clothing he always seemed to be wearing. He insisted on wearing a suit jacket to lectures, despite the informal way they were organised, and underneath he would wear a thick knitted jumper and a shirt at the very least. It gave him a fuller body than expected of his lean face, and made him look slightly like a tortoise. This image was added to by the way his top lip naturally curled over the rest of his mouth. When he smiled however, he seemed to have rows and rows of teeth, like a shark. His eyes were so round he constantly appeared to be in utter disbelief of his surroundings.

'Lucas, we should go for a night together' he said to me. It was probably the first time I had heard him speak. He wasn't one for answering questions in class. I felt I couldn't refuse because his utterance was more a command than an offer.

'Oh, okay, where did you want to go Ma...man' I asked, stumbling over his first name.

'I thought you could show me some place yes?' he said.

'Well the Union... We could go to the bar in the Student's Union'.

'Yes Lucas, I would like that very much' he replied nodding. 'Meet me at the bus stop outside at seven. We will go dancing, fun time'.

Before I could say anything else he left me, waving and smiling with his many teeth. I was not entirely sure what to make of it, and I suddenly realised I had no way to back out of the arrangement because I had no contact details for Madcat. I fully appreciated the irony of our chosen subject of study.

He hadn't given me a telephone number or any other way of contacting him. I didn't know if he lived on campus, or was somehow living elsewhere and commuting in for lectures. I couldn't look him up in the student directory because I couldn't remember his real name because I was so hopelessly small minded. I just had to show up and hope for the best, in the way we all had to when we were little and mobile phones weren't readily available. I took a moment to curse myself for being so ignorant of other cultures.

I got to the bus stop early because I hated the thought of Madcat waiting alone as the sun went down on the empire of our campus. It was only as I got there I realised it was a strange place to meet someone for a night out. Every time a bus drew up the driver assumed I was waiting to leave, because there was only one bus service that passed through campus and the only people usually waiting at the bus stop were waiting for a bus.

I started to get worried Madcat wouldn't show, which would serve as an embarrassing admission for me further down the line. Being jilted at a bus stop would not have been the best conclusion for the evening. I was however sort of hoping he wouldn't turn up because I wasn't sure what I was going to do with him, or what he was expecting. I always find one-on-one guy time a little bit homoerotic and therefore uncomfortable and the fact I barely knew the guy made it seem a bit like a first date. I felt like I should have brought flowers.

It started raining and an older looking boy who had been lurking around outside the bar decided to take cover under the bus shelter with me. I pulled the collar of my suede jacket up to protect my face from the wind which continued to whip across the open front. I hoped it would also serve in making me look more mysterious and cool to the strange new arrival.

He looked at me shiftily, as though he couldn't work me out, not sure if he could trust me. I pulled exactly the same face back, mirroring him. I was there first and wasn't about to be scared off.

Suddenly another boy ran in, out of the rain, a newspaper over his head for protection. He was only wearing a green and white striped football shirt and a pair of jogging bottoms. I automatically assumed he hadn't checked the weather forecast before heading out, or had simply lost track of time in the bar.

'Naz man, sorry I'm late' he said as he shook off the excess rain like a dog.

'That's alright' said the other boy, who must have been Naz.

'How much is it?'

'Special for you my friend, 40 a G'.

'Sweet'.

Money passed hands and then a little cellophane package went back the other way. It seemed weird to me. I wasn't used to seeing things like that so close up. I thought it was the kind of stuff that only ever happened in teen dramas on TV, but there is was, right in my face, in a bus stop.

The boy ran off again, after placing the sodden newspaper back on top of his thinning hair. Naz returned to his seat in the bus stop. I didn't want to look at him in case he offered me some. I struggled to say no to anything, I think the fact I was sat in a bus stop waiting for an Indian boy is testament to that.

I was however, concerned I could start up a drug habit just to be polite. I had never done drugs and I wouldn't have known what I was doing if I were to even consider starting. I kept looking past Naz, to see if Madcat was coming from his direction. The only problem was I worried it would look like I was staring at him. Eventually I settled on just staring straight ahead, out into the road, and beyond it, to the hill upon which the main lecture building was based.

Another boy came out of the rain and shook hands with Naz. I made a conscious effort not to stare but to pay attention out of the corner of my eye.

'How have you been man?' the new boy asked Naz.

'Yeah, pretty good. The usual?'

'Yeah please. How's business?'

'Can't complain. The drought is off at least'.

Something about the way he said it implied he wasn't talking about the weather. I couldn't work out what else it could have meant.

'It weighed up at 3.5, is that cool?'

'Yeah, cheers'.

More money was passed over, and this time a little wrap of silver foil went back. I don't know what the difference in these things is.

'Look, I've got to get over to the flat, the boys are watching *Roadhouse*, and I'm supposed to be cooking dinner'.

'Yeah, safe' said Naz.

I realised I had accidentally started staring at them halfway through the exchange. As a result I had not noticed Madcat was sat on my other side. He was wearing his usual uniform of shirt, knit and blazer.

'Lucas, you wait long?' he asked me, grinning his razor teeth.

'No, I was just… where are we going?'

'To the Union, to make a boogie yes?'

He shook for me, shuddering from the shoulders downwards to indicate what he meant by the word boogie. I could have guessed without the action.

As we got inside I turned to Madcat and asked what he fancied drinking, figuring I would match him because it was what I had been taught to do by a friend. You should always match your guest's drink.

'Coca-Cola' he said.

'Oh. I thought maybe you would fancy something stronger'.

'Stronger?'

'Like alcohol, something alcoholic. Oh, do you drink?'

'No, I do not!'

There was the first in a long line of awkward pauses which would make up the evening.

'Guess I'll have a coke as well then' I said. I felt obliged to get the first round in, not only as a host but also as a result of Madcat's reluctance to walk up to the bar and order. With our bubbling pints of coke and ice in hand we found a table by the door, one of the high ones accompanied by a couple of stools. I sat down with a view of the door so I could nod at or greet anyone I knew as they came in. My hope was I could possibly escape spending the whole evening with Madcat alone. He, however, decided to drag his chair around and sit directly next to me. As such we looked like we were either on a date and getting awfully cosy, as I had initially feared, or we had explicitly set up our chairs with the sole intention of staring at girls as they came in.

I watched Madcat give a couple of them the eye before I realised. He wasn't even subtle. The problem was it wasn't just the eye he was giving them, it was the whole face.

When he saw a girl whose form he found agreeable he would wiggle his big arching eyebrows and his round eyes would pull even wider. He would then grin in a manner so exaggerated that for minutes after I could still see the creases in his cheeks. It was not a good look. I couldn't really say anything though because it wasn't my place to. For all I knew it might have been considered a custom in India, an acceptable form of greeting.

'Shall we do something else?' I asked.

'Shall we dance?'

I looked around the empty bar. Because it was so early there wouldn't be anybody on the dance floor area in the next room, including a DJ. The door wasn't even open. There was just the small bar. I didn't know how to explain that to him.

'Not yet, shall we play pool?'

He agreed and followed me over to the pool table, which luckily for me was available. I put money in and set up the balls. I thought to myself it was only fair I allowed Madcat to make the break, because for some reason I had just assumed when he accepted a game of pool with me he would be capable of playing a game of pool. I was incorrect in this assumption.

He held the hilt of the pool cue and swung the top down hard on top of the triangle of collected red and yellow balls so they dispersed slightly away from the point of impact with a loud crack which caused the lazy-looking barman to glare at us. I quickly rushed around the table, collecting the balls so none would disappear off into a pocket.

I then let him have another go, thinking maybe it had been an accident but he repeated the same move, yielding the same results. I finally relieved him of the duty and took the first shot myself. I managed to pot a yellow, which was a miracle by my standards. Usually I played at a level marginally better than Madcat's.

'Right, you're reds. You have to pot the red balls, okay?' I said. I passed him the only cue. He smiled at me. Luckily it was different to the one he had granted the girls he had seen entering the bar moments before. I smiled back. Our language barrier wasn't that bad after all, I thought to myself. There was always pool, and there was always Coca-Cola.

Madcat held the cue in one hand, straight out before him like a fencing sword and then he swung it down on the table, creating a similar snapping sound to his previous attempts. I realised he was completely unaware my break had been a lesson in how to conduct yourself correctly at a pool table.

The cue clambered against the side of the table and he chased one of the balls along, scooping and sweeping at it with the top quarter of the cue, until it dropped into the pocket. I was reminded of the hook a duck fairground game.

I didn't have the patience to correct him. I was worried he would be upset he had done wrong, so I stood back and let Madcat continue to violently swing the cue down at the red balls until the table was completely clear of them, and then the yellow balls, and then the cue ball. This proved mildly amusing to the group of girls who had gathered something was amiss and were trying not to be obvious about watching and laughing.

'Well done mate' I said and downed my coke.

'Lights come on in other bar, we dance now?' he asked, pointing through the dividing door into Bar Two where the big nights on campus were hosted.

I wasn't sure what kind of event was on, or what kind of music would be played but I could see staff setting up the optics along the back of the bar and a DJ checking the sound system over.

I thought about explaining the protocols of a night out to Madcat, but seeing how he didn't drink I realised he wouldn't be able to understand the concepts of pre-drinking or being fashionably late. Judging by what he wore day in, day out I figured he wouldn't understand getting dressed up either.

'There won't be anyone in there, it's not really kicked off yet. There's no music' I said, gesturing into the empty room with wild hand movements.

Madcat paid no attention. He walked out, across the foyer and into Bar Two. I had no choice but to follow. The lights were a bit of a shock, it was what I imagined being on a tanning bed to feel like.

The only time I ever saw the overhead strip lights on in Bar Two was when they were kicking us out at two or three in the morning. To see it then, as a space with a bar and a raised semi-circular platform around the DJ stand was somewhat disheartening. It ruined the magic. The only thing I could compare it to was when I went to Disneyland and saw Mickey Mouse pad off through a gate, take off his head and light a cigarette.

'Nobody is here' said Madcat.

'Yeah. I tried to tell you that'.

A boy walked in with a pair of headphones round his neck and a large CD carry case under his arm.

'Guys, I'm not starting until at least nine!' he called across to us, his voice echoing in the expanse.

'Yeah, we know' I replied, feeling like I was holding the reins of a toddler. I didn't recognise the DJ, he wasn't the usual one. He was wearing a skinny striped t-shirt and a beanie. It sort of seemed like he had eyeliner on. He looked weird.

'What night is it tonight anyway?' I asked, trying to be causal.

'*Suck My Rock*'.

'What?'

'It's a mix of rock and indie and stuff'.

'Have you got any Avril Lavigne?'

'It's not really that sort of night. I'll see what I can do though' he said before walking off.

I let him get on with his things. While I had been talking to the DJ I had hoped Madcat would take the initiative to get a round in, even if they were only soft drinks. I was out of luck.

'Madcat' I sort of mumbled, feeling sure his name must have been something similar for me to give him the nickname in the first place, 'could you get me a coke?'

He bowed and walked off to the bar. It made me feel terrible. It was like he was serving me. I just thought it was only fair he get me one back because I had got the first ones in and the whole thing had been his idea in the first place. Instead I was left with this hollow, guilty feeling in my chest because of the look on his face and the little bow. It seems silly in hindsight but at the time I needed him to buy me a drink to justify it all to myself.

By the time Madcat returned the lights had gone out. There were the usual disco lights spinning across the floor and people were slowly starting to trickle in. I couldn't say exactly why it took Madcat so long to buy a couple of cokes. I wouldn't really like to dwell on it, to think about what he could have possibly been doing. I wondered what his bar protocol was like. I had seen the way he acted around the women and drug dealers of campus and it wasn't particularly acceptable.

I didn't recognise any of the songs the DJ was playing but at the same time I couldn't sit on the sofa in the corner with Madcat any longer. He had thrown his blazer off down the back and then sat far too close to me, despite the fact the sofa had three different sections for three different bums. He just sat near enough on me and grinned out at the room, jiggling his head to the music.

'Do you want to dance Madcat?' I asked him, forgetting I had made up the name. He shook his head at me. 'Come on'.

I got up. He stayed exactly where he was, still pushed up against where I had been, not daring to shake off his persona and live a little.

I guess I should state I am not the best dancer. This becomes apparent further into the story, not a lot further mind you. It's just worth pointing out because it serves a point. I don't know what to classify as the movements I make when music is played in my vicinity but it isn't dancing. It seems to make people happy, or at least it makes my friends happy, they like watching me dance. I think one of them once said I dance the way a toddler dances when they've had too much sugar. I can't really describe it an awful lot further. It's just quite unique and shouldn't be copied, which is why it became very awkward when Madcat finally stood up, put his drink on the floor and started dancing.

I had been hoping, and again I have to be very careful with my words so I don't come off as a racist, he would do the kind of dancing you see in Bollywood films, with lots of big hand actions and head wiggles. What Madcat actually did was copy my sweet moves exactly. When there is one of you dancing in such a way it can almost be ignored by the majority of people, or seen as being quite sweet. When there are two of you, it becomes harrowing and vaguely threatening.

The vague threat grows when one of the dancers (for serious want of a better word) starts gyrating and grinding against any girl who happens to try and make her way across the filling dance floor on her way to the bar, or a seat, or the toilet, or her friends.

The music kept building as if the DJ knew he was setting the scene for one of the worst dance competitions known to man. A circle of horror began to form around Madcat as he swaggered, ducked, dived and bounced around like he had seen me doing. He would then intermittently aim a thrust of his hips at one of the girls gathered around the circle, lick his lips and begin the whole cycle of moves again.

Rather than turn away in disgust or report him to security the circle of people began clapping, and wolfwhistling, egging him on. Before long even the DJ had stopped focusing on the music and was instead just absorbing the images of the little Indian lad spinning around and air humping the room.

The interest which had accumulated around Madcat's dancing started to turn as soon as he changed his style slightly and included a pinching movement. This he would employ on any part of a girl he chose as he bopped around the cage of people. He probably thought it was a way of making his intentions known, like when a dog pisses on a tree to mark it's territory. Giving a girl a little grab on the buttock or the breast was probably completely acceptable where he was from, but it wasn't going down too well in the Student's Union. There was a very real danger I was about to be thrown into the lion's den as an accomplice to his crimes. I needed out.

Just in the nick of time I spotted a couple of my friends stood at the bar. They, like everyone else, had turned to watch what was going on in the pit, and where it would lead. Nobody knew what the outcome would be but they were all waiting for someone else to take the first step over the line, which would progress the whole scene into hysteria.

I hid between them, worried I had left this alien at the whim of the scientists. I felt I had failed him like when

Elliott finds E.T. in a ditch and he has gone all white like an old dog poo.

I was hit with a stark realisation. The only thing I could do was get the hell out of there before it could get nasty, before it reached the terrible conclusion his actions were bound to set about. I had an obligation to take the artist formerly known as Madcat with me. I had to keep him safe. He was basically my guest and I was feeding him to the wolves. I shouldered my way through the crowd and found him, red-faced and sweating in his thick knitwear and shirt combination.

'Madcat, it's time to go!' I yelled over the range of voices and distorted music.

'Okay' he replied, still jumping up and down on his mime pogo stick, using my shoulders to get more leverage so he could shoot up in the air, above the circle of the crowd.

'As in now' I screamed, 'I'm going home now!'

'Okay, I come' he said.

I ignored what it sounded like to me, and busted out the other side of the group like a swimmer breaking the calm surface of the water. I looked back and Madcat was gripped tightly to me, like a Bush Baby holding onto the soft underbelly of it's mother, eyes wide with confusion and fear.

The circle of people belched us out and turned, waiting to see what he would do next. Madcat wasn't ready to be the centre of attention anymore. He had seen enough late night revelry and enough of the student life. I could tell all this by the clammy hands which gripped onto my arm like he was undergoing electroshock treatment. He was genuinely scared. The mob mentality had got to him.

Maybe it had brought on a panic attack or a deeply repressed memory. Maybe it had reminded him of the stampede scene in *The Lion King*.

I picked up his jacket from where it had been discarded carelessly down the back of the sofa and then walked outside, with Madcat still tied to my side. The change in atmosphere was dramatic and under the spotlights suspended along the front of the building I could finally fully see the fear. His hair was clinging to his forehead with sweat and his eyes were as wide as ever. He was breathing heavily. It was like he expected to be attacked at any moment, his shoulders were hunched up, ready to tuck his head down into the shell of his body.

'Do you need me to walk you home?' I asked. He nodded slowly, looking into my eyes with the kind of appreciation people are careful never to exhibit.

We started on the route towards St John's but he was still clung to my arm like he was my date, using me as an umbrella or jamboree.

'Where do you actually live?' I asked. He pointed in the direction we were walking, so with him attached like a trophy wife we made our way across the grass to the first set of flats.

'Do you want to come in for a drink?' he asked. I couldn't stand the thought of another Coca-Cola, which I assumed was the only thing he would ever possibly drink, won over by the constant advertising campaigns they ran.

'No Madcat, it's fine'.

I had managed to balance his blazer on his shoulders, and in the fresh air they were not heaving quite as much as they had been moments before.

'Are you sure you will be alright?'

'Are you sure you don't want a drink?' he asked again, holding up his flat key as though it were the promised beverage.

'I really have to go. I've got lectures early tomorrow morning'. I knew this was a complete lie, and just after I said it I realised Madcat also knew it was a complete lie because we were in the same class. It could only have been down to what he had just experienced that he wasn't able to make the connection and was therefore unable to correct me, or call me out over the lie.

I automatically turned and walked away, hoping the action would be read by Madcat for what it was, the end of our time together. Madcat made no attempt to head inside. I turned back to check once I was twenty feet away and he was still staring after me with his big, sad eyes. I waved. He waved back. I walked on. As I went to turn the corner I heard the crunch of gravel behind me. Turning around I realised Madcat was following me.

'I said I'm alright' I shouted, waving again. 'I will see you tomorrow'. Again he returned the wave but continued walking behind me, albeit slightly slower. I started to speed up and as I turned another corner, and was on the home straight I broke out into a run. I stuffed my hands into my jeans pocket and fumbled around for my key. I tried to jam it in the front door but in the panic of it all I couldn't wedge the right key in the lock. I could hear him approaching, slow but terrifying, like Jason Voorhes or a zombie.

I finally got my hand secure on the key and jammed it upright into the lock. I slipped inside, and closed the door quickly and as quietly as possible behind me. I then cut the light in the hall.

Hiding in the shadows I watched Madcat slowly walk past, trying to work out how I could have disappeared completely. It was weird, I was stood panting in my own blacked out hallway, feeling somewhat worse for wear, hiding from a boy who was inexplicably tailing me, and the whole thing started because I changed course.

Monopoly

MICHAEL
October 2008

As I flicked the indicator up I had absolutely no idea what was in store for the evening. I had a strange kind of awkwardness in my belly, which was nothing unusual. It was just returning to campus, and knowing I wasn't *there* anymore, that life was continuing after I had graduated, even if my life didn't seem to be. There were people I felt I had known so well who were continuing with their adventures while it felt I was stuck outside of it all, just getting the occasional glimpse of the things I was missing.

The boys open invitation at the start of the autumn term had turned to 'hurry the fuck up' within that last week. I was sure it was because they were short on food and probably intellectual company. I took the all too familiar slip road, Junction 17 of the M25 and gradually put my foot down on the brake as I approached the roundabout. In the hour drive from home to campus I had smoked three cigarettes and was listening to *Up The Bracket* for the second time through. I took the first exit off the roundabout and followed the dual carriageway to the end, still having to take myself through the steps like I had the first time I had driven solo to University at the age of eighteen.

I was coming up on 22, still didn't have a car or insurance in my own name, and was hopelessly single. Taking a right at the roundabout at the bottom I squinted through my glasses and out the windscreen at the row of shops on the corner, trying to ascertain if the corner shop was open for me to pick up some dinner and amenities. I was lucky, it was. I had tried to judge times that Friday evening on the basis that I didn't want to get stuck in rush hour traffic, but I also didn't want to arrive too late and ruin the chance of having a good evening with my boys, I had got the balance just right it seemed.

I pulled my brother's Ford Fiesta up to the curb just outside and took a deep breath at the sight of what I would earlier in life have described as 'bigger boys', a group of teenagers, stood about with BMXs and probably concealed weapons. It always takes a while for me to register the fact I don't need to fear them anymore, that I'm an adult and have the powers of deduction and reason on my side. I got out, suave as possible, locked the door behind me and started on my way in but they were slightly blocking the path.

'Excuse me' I said as I walked through, their shoulders brushed aside by my elbows.

'Excuse yourself, you curly haired fuck'.

I didn't have a comeback, I hadn't expected it. I *had* excused myself, and I do have curly hair.

I went inside and walked back and forth over the two aisles of food, trying to remember exactly what students eat, and whether I should turn up with enough shopping to last the four of them a week when I could barely afford to do anything for myself still, because eventually overdrafts do need to be paid back. I settled on a selection of Pot Noodles, tinned food, packets of biscuits, crisps and chocolate (for munchies purposes), two bottles of Coke and I got myself another pack of Marlboro Lights. In the boot of the car was a bottle of Appleton Estate Jamaican rum, which I had procured through completely legitimate means earlier that week. I decided I would offer it up as a present to the boys, along with my presence and my other gifts of food and good times.

My purchases were tossed into two pathetic blue and white striped bags and I headed back outside. Luckily the naughty children had disappeared. I got back in the car, spun it around and headed through the housing estate. I passed the traffic calming bollards, which Oliver's ex girlfriend had once driven over drunk and completely destroyed. They still looked slightly angled. It made me smile for some reason.

From there I began up the hill, where the grassy banks stuck up like dead men's noses and the road narrowed to near enough a single lane. I came round the corner and saw the spot where a year and a half before Oliver and a girl had been in a serious road accident. The surrounding woodland had never really recovered and I was sure I could see the exact spot where the car had caught on the hill, and flipped back out into the road, skidding on it's roof. It still sent a shiver through me. It didn't matter how many times he laughed it off, the fact of the matter was we very nearly lost him, and it would have closed down a lot of our behavior a lot sooner if it had happened.

With the accident site behind me the road began to open out again and I kept the fingers of my left hand pressed up ready to indicate when I saw the sign for campus. It didn't matter how many times I journeyed up that same road, the turning always jumped out at me.

I came past the 'tradesman's entrance' which was used by visiting football teams to access the fields where they would thoroughly ruin *our* team; Oldham Park. Beyond, the path was completely surrounded by trees. It was like driving through a continuing halo of foliage. I was taken back to the first time I had visited the campus. It had been autumn then as well.

We, being my parents and I, had started our visit on the other campus in the local town. I remember having a stinking hangover as a result of another night out, and I took the town campus to be just another concrete deathtrap where I would feel completely cold and alone for three years.

I had spent far too many weekends being driven to different corners of the country, to different campuses and I'd had enough. I realise how extremely ungrateful that makes me sound but it's something I have come to terms with. We were told Law, Business and Nursing students would be based on the other campus so were driven out in one of the University's minibuses. As we came through the tree-lined alley and onto the drive, I knew it was where I wanted to do my degree, where I could see myself spending my time.

A few months later I was invited up for an open day with other potential students. It was there I met Zara who served as a friend and brief fancy in the opening weeks of my fresher year. The important thing for me during the open day was the thought of being there comfortably, of just existing.

I decided the best way to test whether I could handle it was to break away from the group, to disappear off from the tour and just try being a student for a while. So in my worn Converse high tops and my corduroy jacket I didn't turn up at 14:30 for the 'Library Orientation' session but instead sat in the cafeteria area with a cappuccino, a packet of cigarettes and a copy of Rolling Stone magazine, just taking in the ambience.

When my parents came later that day to pick me up I told them I could see myself being there. I lived that afternoon of ignoring my duties and bunking off from what I was supposed to be doing for three full years.

I caught the indicator with the index finger of my left hand and pulled onto the long driveway that eventually met with the front of the Manor House. Before I could get to that point however, was the security booth, a place I was far too familiar with.

I instantly thought of evenings returning to campus in minibuses and taxis, making a nuisance of ourselves before heading off into the night or even to bed. It reminded me of nights crawling through the undergrowth with Lisa in full camouflage gear pretending we were ninjas.

I slowed over the three sets of speed bumps and simultaneously searched my pocket for my wallet. Locating it I then searched my wallet for my expired ID card in the hope I could fake my way through like The Doctor, rather than have Oliver, Eli, Ross or Danny have to walk up to meet me.

As I came in sight of the security booth I just smiled and waved my ID. The barrier raised and I was in.

I felt like a master thief.

I had broken into Gringotts.

I was back in the vault of campus.

I was home.

I was somewhat overwhelmed by what I was seeing. It is always weird returning to somewhere which previously meant so much to you for so long. I was seeing it from different eyes, from a different place in life. I felt so happy and so sad at the same time. On the right was the bar and refectory where I had danced and vomited on too many an occasion. Beyond were the block of flats I had lived in during my time in St John's and on my left was the library where I had never spent as much time as I should have done, despite my good intentions.

The shadow of the Manor House loomed over my little car and I turned off towards St Christopher's Halls of Residence, coming past the gym, and the upturned tree that was still lying in the same spot it always had and would, turning off towards the car park.

The place seemed quiet, unusually so for a Friday night, or for the memory of a Friday night I had. The few people I did see I didn't recognise. It was a strange new sensation. There had been a time when I couldn't have stepped out the door without running into someone I had at the very least enjoyed a pint with, and here I was faced with total strangers. It was all starting to get a little bit *Wicker Man* as I pulled up on the stony car park and got out.

Juggling the two bags of shopping and my little suitcase on wheels I started back down the way I had come, heading for their flat, a space Oliver, Ross, Eli and Danny would never and could never give up to anyone else.

Somehow I lit a cigarette and made my way up the grate stairs, up two floors to the door I didn't have a key for anymore. Before I knocked I smoked the rest of my cigarette and just looked out, enjoying the view again. The sky had gone to purple in my arriving moments and I was now faced with an evening of expectations and the unknown. I wasn't sure what the boys would be like as third years. I also wasn't sure how many people on campus would be pleased to see me. The concept of who had been first, second and third year students during my time all merged, I couldn't work out who had left, who had graduated, who still liked me, who I still liked and whether I cared.

I glanced across at the other door the balcony at the top of the stairs led to, a door I had knocked on plenty of occasions previously when I had conducted a strange relationship with one of the girls who had lived there. I had upset her too many times and it had all exploded in my face. With hindsight I regretted my bold decisions to paint myself as a cad and a vagabond.

I threw my cigarette overboard where it fell and joined the league of others. I knocked on the door, took a deep breath and then the colour came back into my life.

'Wait, no, I'll get it' I heard Ross scream from behind the door.

'Well are you going?' shouted Eli in response.

I stood and waited.

'Ross, just open the door'.

I waited longer.

'I'm coming, wait a second'.

I rang the bell again.

'I said I was coming, I might just leave you out there'.

'Ross, just answer the fucking door'.

'Alright, no need to get so *testes*'.

The door swung open and Ross grabbed at me, pulling me up on my toes and over the threshold into a hug.

'I've missed you baby' he crooned in my tiny ear.

'Get off!' I yelled as he tried to lick me with his lizard tongue.

'Put him down, he's mine' called Oliver, sauntering down the hallway. Ross immediately obeyed, settling me back on my feet, but giving one side of my face a horrible caress with his clammy palm.

'Come here you delicious bastard' said Oliver, picking me up once more. 'Don't ever leave me again' he added, and I had no intention of doing so, I was in for the foreseeable. A door suddenly opened, and Danny stepped out.

'Hey dude, how's it going?' he asked, grabbing my free hand, the one that wasn't trapped between me and Oliver.

'Good thanks' I muffled.

Another door opened, which in my time had led to Ross's room, complete with *Back To The Future* poster and fake tan ruined mattress. Eli stepped out.

'There's my boy' he yelled and jumped on Oliver's back to try and get a grip of my hair or something, so he could feel a part of it. They eventually relinquished their hold and stepped back to look at me, to see if I had changed, to see if I was a grown up. It was like I had flown back to Never Neverland.

'It's good to be back boys' I said. They picked up the shopping, picked up my bag, picked up me and deposited the lot in the kitchen which looked very much how I had left it with one obvious exception.

'We've got a sofa!' yelled Ross, as if I couldn't see the awkward-looking brown felt couch, on spindly metal legs, up against the wall.

'I can see that'.

'It's your bed' said Ross, well aware of my penchant for falling flat out unconscious on the worn out carpet. As a mark of solidarity my brother had chosen to pass out in exactly the same spot once, when he had come to visit me, and consumed too many special brownies.

'Cool, thanks' I said. There was a moment of calm, an almost awkward pause. I worried I had in fact moved on in those few short months, that somehow we didn't have as many things in common as I thought, as though the scene had changed, and I had been left outside in the cold.

'What did you bring us then?'

The question brought the ridiculous notion I had been left out crashing to the floor and we were back on form again. It was needed. Everyone jumped to action. They rifled through the plastic bags, pulling out the food I had brought them. They put the coke in the fridge, piled the food up on the side ready for after a smoke and then they turned on me again.

'Did you not bring any alcohol? We need it for the game tonight. We've only got a case of Biere Speciales'

'Come on, what do you take me for?' I asked, unzipping my suitcase and pulling the bottle of rum out. They let up a collective roar. It was as though I were presenting a newborn king.

'Eli invented a game, tell him about the game!' Ross yelled, getting too excited for a moment. He was bouncing off the walls and table.

'Calm down dog!' Oliver said. 'You are in for a treat tonight Michael, we've invented our own drinking game'.

'Your own?'

'Yeah!'

'How does that work?'

'Well, what's the one thing missing from Monopoly?'

'Probably all the little red hotels you've stuck up your arse' I replied.

'Funny. No. Drinking!'

'So you've invented…'

'Drinking Monopoly' they shouted in chorus and burst into a flurry of activity, as though they were choreographed. A chair was pulled out for me. The table was cleared with a quick shift of everything to the floor, and then the Monopoly board was brought down right in front of me. On top of the box one of them placed an A4 sheet of rules in Oliver's almost too beautiful handwriting:

DRINKING MONOPOLY RULES

1. Drink two fingers when you land on someone's property
2. Drink two fingers when you roll a double and make up a rule
3. Drink two fingers when you land on GO
4. If you go to JAIL we play Waterfall[1] (with the jailed going last)
5. Drink two fingers when you buy a house, four fingers if you buy a hotel
6. Drink two fingers when you land on TAX
7. Drink rest of drink if you land on FREE PARKING (everyone else cheers and takes a tip)
8. Drink two fingers if you land on WATERWORKS
9. Drink one finger when you take a CHANCE card
10. If you land on COMMUNITY CHEST nominate someone to drink two fingers
11. Drink however many fingers you rolled on that turn if you land on ELECTRIC
12. If you land on MAYFAIR then it is Gentleman's Rules[1]
13. Drink two fingers if you violate any of the rules
14. If you have to pay a fine you drink one sip for each £100 spent

---

[1] Waterfall is a separate drinking game in itself where everyone starts with a full glass/bottle/can. The first person at the circle starts drinking, then the second joins in and so on. The first person cannot stop drinking until everyone in the circle is drinking.
[1] Gentleman's Rules are: no swearing, no pointing, no elbows on tables, no first names, no slang and no cheating

I was amazed. I had never seen them work so hard on anything.

'Who's idea was this?'

'Well we all contributed but it's Eli's brainchild really' said Oliver, offering up the stage for Eli, who took it gladly.

'What made you think of that?'

'Well Monopoly is notoriously boring' he said.

'Right...'

'And drinking is brilliant'.

'Right...'

'So they should balance each other out'.

'Right...'

'And we should be in for a pleasant evening'.

They all took a seat, placed the Chance cards and the Community Chest cards in the appropriate positions and then laid the rules so we could all read them.

'I'm the dog' screamed Ross, clutching the piece from where Eli had carefully placed it on the Start square with the others.

'We know' said Eli.

'I'll be the thimble' said Oliver, as nonchalant as possible.

'Fuck off' said Eli, 'I want to be the thimble'.

'What's so special about the thimble?' I asked.

'It's just the nicest one' said Oliver as though it was the most obvious thing in the world.

'Well I'll be the thimble then, just to resolve the conflict' I said, desperate for the thimble.

'You can't just walk in here and demand the thimble!' Eli said raising his voice. I was instantly reminded of the scene in Goodfellas where Joe Pesci gets pissed off about being called funny.

'Look guys, I'm going to be the top hat' said Danny, taking another piece out of the equation. It was like watching a game of Russian Roulette in a Vietnamese prisoner of war camp.

'Alright, I'll be the fucking ship' said Oliver bowing out.

'I'll be the racing car' I conceded.

'Yes, fucking thimble' Eli said.

'Just don't jam it up your arse' I replied, still bitter apparently.

'It's not a Twix!' responded Eli.

'Who wants a Biere Speciale' asked Oliver and the game began.

Danny rolled first, prompted by Eli with a comment of 'age before beauty', which was ridiculous given how pretty Danny is. He rolled a six, as two threes.

'You rolled a double, there's a rule for that' said Eli, scanning down the list with his finger.

'Is it *drink*?' I asked.

'No, it is; drink two fingers when you roll a double and make up a rule. What's your rule Danny?'

'Right,' he said, looking around the room for inspiration, 'whoever rolls a double has to put the mop on the floor, put their forehead on the top of the mop handle and run around it ten times'.

There was a collective cheer, it was a good rule. I rolled next under the age before beauty rule and made it to Whitechapel Road.

'What does that mean?' I asked.

'Drink!' said Danny.

'Yeah, but wait, there's a rule' Eli said, running his finger down the list.

'Come on, I'm thirsty'.

'Drink two fingers'.

'Is that it?'

'Yeah, you just wait'.

Oliver rolled next.

'Fuck, a double, what do I do now?' he asked, forgetting the rules established just two rolls before.

'You get to make a rule' said Danny.

'Not just yet' said Eli, the fucking Gamesmaster. 'First, you must spin round the mop'.

'Oooooh!' we all said.

'Don't sweat it boys, I've got this' said Oliver, picking up the mop, and heading out onto the linoleum of the joined kitchen area. He pushed all the rubbish to one side so he had a good bit of space, a dance floor for his spinning act and we just had to count.

Oliver rested his right hand on the top of the mop and placed his left hand a quarter of the way down the shaft, he put his head down on his clenched right hand, took a deep breath and started.

'One'.

Oliver made a wide circle of the broom, his socked feet padding against the floor.

'Two'.

He let out a slight screech, but maintained his position.

'Three'.

He got the hang of what he was doing, and pushed on, a new determination in his heavy steps.

'Four'.

His left foot swung out wildly and he steadied himself before continuing.

'Five'.

Oliver gathered speed and looked like he was leaning heavier on the head of the mop.

'Six'.

'I think I'm going to be sick' he called out to us, closing his eyes against the waves that hit him as he span.

'Seven'.

We were all out of our chairs, cheering at him with each revolution round the floored mop.

'Eight'.

He had found his pace, like a marathon runner, slow and steady wins the race.

'Nine'.

He lost his footing, and before any of us could move from our upright positions round the table he careened over and caught his brow on the corner of the worktop, before falling to the floor and collapsing on his back.

'Wow, that doesn't look safe at all' said Eli. He definitely had a point. None of us moved.

'Ahhhhhhh!' said Oliver.

'Maybe we should stop guys' I suggested.

'No!' said Danny.

'Ahhhhhhhh!' said Oliver.

'We'll just spot each other, like they do with gymnasts'.

'Maybe we should all take our socks off' said Ross.

'Ahhhhhhhhh!' said Oliver.

'Why?' asked Danny.

'For grip' replied Ross.

'Ahhhhhhhhhh!' said Oliver.

'Yeah, that's probably not a bad idea' said Eli.

'Does anyone need another beer?' asked Danny.

'Ahhhhhhh!' said Oliver.

'Whose go is it?' asked Ross.

'Yours' I said.

'Oh right' he replied, 'come on Oli, it's my go, get up'.

'Ahhhhhhh!' said Oliver.

We all looked down at him, he had both hands pressed over his left eye, which had narrowly avoided being split open *Une Chien Andalou* style.

'Yeah, guys, I'm not spinning on the mop' said Eli.

'Yeah, actually, can I change my rule?' asked Danny.

'Fuck off' said Oliver, sitting up again, 'you're all doing that!'

'Right, can I roll now?' said Ross.

'I hope you get a double' said Oliver, pulling himself up and returning to his seat.

'Wait, Oli, you need to set another rule for a double first' said Eli, who was so proud of the rules he had drawn up that he wasn't going to let anyone drop one.

'Okay, whoever rolls a double has to lick my fucking arsehole'.

'Come on Oli, don't cheapen the game. Also, two fingers for swearing'.

'Here's your two fingers' Oliver said, flicking the V's at Eli. 'Alright, my rule is; a coin is flipped and you have to decide if it is heads or tails, if you get it *wrong* you have to drink. If you get it *right* then the onus moves onto the next person who is then playing for their two fingers plus the previous persons so they would have to drink four if they got it wrong, and so on until we're all fucked and fuck each other'.

'Four fingers for swearing'.

'I thought it was two'.

'You said fuck twice'.

'Two fingers for fuck' Oliver responded quickly. Eli drunk. Oliver drunk. I kept quiet for fear I would have to drink.

'Can I roll now?' asked Ross who was still palming the sweaty dice.

'You may' said Oliver.

Ross didn't even roll a double, and he ended up joining me on Whitechapel Road.

'Fancy getting a flat together?' he asked me.

'Do you know how this game works?'

'Not really, just do as I'm told' he replied.

'Drink' said Eli.

Ross drunk.

'This is going to be fun' said Eli.

It wasn't long before the case of beers was completely gone and we had to move onto the Appleton Estate, which everyone agreed was the most lavish thing they'd had in the flat all year. I hadn't really thought about it, but during my time as a student it had been a steady diet of *Vodkat* or *Glen's* vodka so my offering was something completely exotic and new to them.

The dirty and odd pint glasses were taken down from the cupboards, a different collection to those that had been there during my time as a student but obtained through the same means, by hiding them inside jackets on the way out of the bar after a night out. These glasses were then a third filled with rum and topped up with the Coke, which had been chilled in the fridge since my arrival, our own version of Bollinger.

The drinks were certainly a lot stronger than the beers we had been on, but it wasn't necessarily a good thing. Despite how impressed they had initially been with the high-class quality of a bottle of Appleton Estate, it didn't change the fact it tasted like shit.

'This tastes like shit' I said.

'Two fingers for swearing' said Eli, pointing at me.

'No pointing, two fingers' said Ross.

'Is that a rule?'

'Yeah?' said Ross.

'Nobody is on Mayfair yet' said Eli.

'I'll add it'.

'You can't just add it, wait your turn'.

Eli rolled the dice and got a double.

'Add my rule' said Ross.

'No! My rule is when you roll a two you have to do ten press-ups-'.

'Ooooh' we said, terrified at the thought of exercise.

'With...' he added, 'your trousers down'.

There was a revered hush that came over us; I was reminded of a time in that same spot years before when Eli had said something equally questionable.

I am firmly of the belief you can never really know a man until you've watched him from the gooch up, perform ten press ups with his trousers down. I can safely say I know Oliver, Eli, Ross and Danny, and I can sadly say they know me.

One by one we rolled the dice, took the necessary sips of drink, made up the necessary rules and then passed the hassle onto someone else. Before long we weren't even able to talk to one another, it was just a distorted series of noises aimed in any one particular direction.

'I'm a nurrr be haslam'.

'Na ya mer simba'.

'Yoi fuckin blarsterd, prink'.

Eventually I rolled a double and everyone snapped back to attention like they had electrodes on their nipples.

'Ten spins!' they cried, as I tentatively tried to kiss the smallest amount of rum and coke possible into my mouth.

'I know' I said, getting up and trying to remember what a mop was, and how my legs worked.

'Woah, woah, woah' said Oliver, 'I'm not having him getting hurt. We'll spot him like he's a gymnast'.

As I assumed the position in the middle of the kitchen, with my hands on the mop and my head dangling just above the summit, Oliver and Danny stood up and circled me, making sure if I didn't make the full ten spins, which was highly likely, they would be in place to stop me cracking my skull open in the name of gentlemanly pursuits.

I started my spins slowly, deciding to stand square with the mop and sidestep round it rather than just running rings around it like Oliver had tried to do.

'One, two, three…'.

I lost all concept of where Danny was stood, where Oliver was stood, where it was safe to fall, and where I had gone so spectacularly wrong in life to be spinning around a mop in the kitchen of a third floor flat in a secluded campus in the home counties. It didn't compute.

'Four, five, six…'.

A horrible acidic sickness suddenly hit the back of my throat, and I tried to push it away from my head, but it stuck with the force of the spin, like I was on a carnival ride.

'Seven'.

I felt my feet give way, and I stumbled sideways. I heard a sudden gasp before Oliver's arms reached around my stomach and pulled me in, away from the fridge I had somehow been running for.

'Fuck, that was close' said Oliver.

Never had a truer word been spoken. He slowly placed me back on my feet, brushing me down as though I had been in a snowstorm.

'Two fingers for swearing' said Eli.

'Fuck off' said Oliver.

'Four fingers'.

Oliver cut his losses and returned to the table where he downed his glass of rum and coke.

'That's it, we can't play this anymore. I'm not risking Michael's face'.

With little further consideration he slid his hand under the Monopoly board and flipped everything onto the floor.

'I was winning!' screamed Ross.

'You didn't know what was going on!' Oliver screamed back at him before storming off to his room.

As his parting words echoed down the hall we all took stock of what was going on. We were raised and hunched like primates, ready to turn on each other as confetti money fell between us.

Survival of the fittest.

Dog eat dog.

Remove the head, destroy the brain.

I realised it was entirely true, and as Eli kicked the still fluttering rainbow notes and the bent up plastic houses and hotels to the corner of the room, all I wanted to do was curl up on the uncomfortable sofa and get good and lost in my dreams of a better tomorrow.

One by one the others drifted off to their bedrooms. I felt sad my time as a fully-fledged student was over, but all the worse for knowing they would soon have to join me in the outside world, where getting drunk on a Monday wasn't the done thing, and you couldn't sleep in until Countdown.

With nothing but my thoughts I realised my head was still spinning from my attempt around the mop. I dashed out of the kitchen and carefully vomited into the pube-lined porcelain of the toilet before passing out.

Where Did All The Money Go?

*An essay
on the
terrible things
I did to get by*

It's a question asked of me far too often, and one I don't really have a particular answer for, but in the impossible style I was taught in my three years of higher education I will attempt to make a statement, provide evidence and then follow up with an explanation because four years since I graduated I am still making monthly payments to the loan company, and estimate I will be for the next decade.

In many ways it was the most reckless I have ever been, and I don't just mean financially.

I did things I would never have done.

I took risks I never would have taken.

I got hurt and I hurt others and I got drunk and I got high, and I laughed and I cried....

What an afternoon that was.

The important thing to remember is you shouldn't judge students ever, or group them, because everyone has a different journey, and everyone has different adventures and deep down, you know if you are tutting at a group in a coffee shop, or an individual dragging their coat in the dirt as they pretend they are heading for the library that deep down, underneath it all, you are just jealous, or at the very least highly interested, and that is why you are still reading.

There is a lot to be taken from it, but this is by no means a definitive recollection. This is just mine, all mine, and I hope there is some kind of mirroring aspect for you, because you should enjoy yourself sometimes.

The first issue I would like to address is food.

I had a massive problem with food, and in many ways I still struggle with it. I know a lot of people who managed to put on weight while they were at uni, or their weight would fluctuate. I was quite the opposite.

I found food, especially square meals, were the first thing to disappear from my life as the bank account dwindled back into negative figures. I discovered I could get by on one meal a day, and more often than not there would be no fresh fruit or vegetables involved in that one meal.

I wouldn't have been surprised if I had gone for a blood test and been told I had rickets or scurvy, I lived like a pirate in more ways than one.

I went through phases with food. I would obsessively consume the same thing, day after day and not really think about the content or the nutritional value. I experimented with only eating cheese toasties, with only eating fish fingers, with only eating boil in the bag rice with tins of beans. I tried living on tortilla chips. One week I can remember just eating a giant watermelon, which I kept on my desk with a carving knife stabbed through the top of it.

It was a horrible way to be and I shouldn't have been so surprised I struggled to make it to the majority of my 9am lectures because I must have had no energy at all. I can remember being told by my friend (known in this collection as Harry) if I didn't start eating properly I was going to start losing my hair. Somehow that got through to me, because underneath it all I am a vain and narcissistic creature and the thought of losing my beautiful curls is just too much for me to take!

The only advantage I can possibly think of is girls were always looking to mother me and feed me up. I have lost count of the number of gratis meals I got to enjoy just because I looked like an orphaned puppy. I always felt like I was using these girls, in the way I feel I am using everyone, which in turn is why I try so hard, sometimes too hard with people I like, and why I am always offering up gifts of writing and music and love. It's my way of giving back for anything I perceive to be taking. I feel I could and should take this opportunity to thank anyone who ever cooked for me during those days. I was helpless and you were far too kind.

There was a time when I could squeeze myself into a pair of women's size eight jeans, which according to Google places my waist at around the 25-inch mark, which is apparently the same as Jennifer Ellison.

Things got so bad in my third year I only had around ten pounds a week for shopping, and this would invariably go on a big bag of pasta, something resembling meat, and then the rest would be spent on frozen goods and chocolate. That was my money gone and my food sorted for the week.

I would return home at the end of term to find the plates of food put down in front of me were ridiculously big, compared to what I had been eating. I had managed to shrink my stomach.

I got into a habit of drinking black coffee all day, with at least one sugar, and then smoking at least twenty roll ups. I found this would cease my hunger pains until the early afternoon.

When I was working on an essay I would be locked in my room for eight to twelve hours just existing, desperately trying to get finished so I could go out to play.

Anyone who visited me would have to deal with the smog I emitted, and the fact I would only ever be dressed in a pair of ragged three quarter length shorts. This was how I managed to get by.

You might be pleased to know I have since got a much better respect for food. I can remember my Grandma (God bless her) once said I 'ate to live' while the rest of the family 'lived to eat'. I am afraid this is still the case. I only put food into my body with the express purpose that if I don't then I won't be able to do all of the things I want, and that worryingly, I might lose my hair.

I've recently starting exercising properly, running and other bits of cardio, so I am watching what I eat in a positive way.

I've also got a girlfriend who can make absolutely anything taste incredible, and her love of food is contagious so I have learnt to cook, and to take pride in the presentation of food, and to indulge a bit every now and then, and it's pretty good, but I will always remember there was a time when I was probably borderline eating disorder.

Seeing how I have mentioned smoking already I may as well continue on that avenue. I am now near enough clear of smoking. I still get pulled in every now and then when I have had a little too much to drink but for the most part I won't allow myself to smoke for two major reasons.

The first is I hate anything having control over me, other than myself. I'm too wrapped up in myself to want to smoke, and that is quite a pleasant thing to feel.

The second is the sheer cost of it. There was a time when I could buy a pack of ten fags for just over two quid, and they would do me for a week. Then you finish school and you're at college, where there is a designated smoking area, and then you hit eighteen and you are out drinking, and at that time you could still smoke indoors. I went up to ten, and then twenty a day. The prices kept going up and were just under the seven pound mark for twenty when I quit.

We used to smoke in the Wimpy in Rayleigh high street when we were done with our GCSE exams for the day. That wasn't even long ago. They had one side of the room designated smoking and the other was considered non-smoking but there was no attempt to divide beyond that. The smoke had no regard for these imaginary borders and if you didn't finish your food quick enough then it would taste like five people smoking at you. It was a horrible way to do things.

When the smoking ban came in I was working in a pub (which may or may not have inspired some of the earlier stories), and I can remember my joy at not having to empty the ashtrays at the end of the night. We had a metal bucket we would throw the ash and debris in and then wash the glass ashtrays up using an old paintbrush. The stink that came off of it was almost enough to make me quit right there.

I smoked the whole time I was at university, and thinking about it now I cannot understand how I managed when I didn't even have enough money for food. There was just always a way of smoking. On more than one occasion I went through the butts in the ashtray in my room, collected up all the odd bits of tobacco I could find and smoked it in a rizla. It was something I learnt from reading Orwell's *Down And Out In Paris And London* but which I have found out since isn't uncommon for homeless people to do.

Despite the fact I never seemed to have any money I can remember getting high an awful lot. There are a number of stories which casually mention drug use within this collection in fact. I can only assume this was down to the generosity of other people. I don't know what I was doing to be included in a share of the smoke but it served me well and I thank you all.

Some of the best and worst times involved having a communal smoke, and I recently compared the smoking of a joint amongst friends as being the equivalent of passing a peace pipe around the tribe. There's something very beautiful and very bonding about the experience, and I feel close to anyone I have ever smoked with.

I would also like to address the idea of alcohol or how I managed to always be pissed, or a lot of the time at least, when I literally didn't have any money. In my first year I was out far too much and it always seemed to end in disaster, as many of the stories of the time will allude to. If you were to ask my flatmates during that year they would tell you the kind of japes I got into. I can remember, well I can't, but I was told about it enough times, the night of my nineteenth birthday.

My brother had come up to stay. He must have been sixteen at the time, and was much cooler and better with his drink than me. I managed to drink myself into a stupor and I believe I was thrown out of the Student's Union for being sick. As I was leaving, or being escorted out, I yelled out for my brother and he quickly ran out to me, informed me he had met a girl and was probably going to head back to hers, and then left me to it.

I made it back to my flat, made it to bed, and seemed to be okay. At around three in the morning my flatmates were awoken by a clanging sound. Pushing my bedroom door open they found me wobbling back and forth, hitting a bin full of my own sick against the walls like I was in a pinball machine. They guided me to the bathroom, cleaned me up, and then put me back to bed. There were many nights like that.

By the time I got into my second year I had found a firm set of friends and had hit a stride with my drinking habits. I would still regularly overindulge and fall down in the street but it was different.

I started performing at the Open Mic nights in the Union on a Monday, where the reward for getting up and playing three songs was a bottle of Jackrabbit wine, which I would drink from a pint glass, and then attempt to get up to play another set, and earn another bottle.

Those second sets were never quite as fluid as the first, and I would sit grinning at my would-be audience with a fuzzy head and claret-stained teeth.

This became a stable way of getting pissed for absolutely nothing. By that point I could hammer a few songs of my own together along with covers by Pixies, Radiohead, Bob Dylan, The Libertines, Placebo, Bob Marley and David Bowie. These made up my set and got me used to the fact if you get up in front of an audience with an acoustic guitar they are going to make you work really fucking hard for approval. I had my friends, and they were fans, or at least they clapped, but for the most part the event was met with contempt by the rest of the student body. Around this time was also my first experience of being in a band, a temperament I have tried to match many times since.

Aside from the red, red wine I also developed a taste for gin, vodka and rum, albeit never all at once. I don't know whether I worked out these were the spirits available in cheaper supermarket own brand versions, or if I genuinely thought I liked them. I had some amazing nights with a hip flask of rum, or a small bottle of vodka or gin, just in and around campus. I can remember one night which I believe is alluded to in my novel *Situation One* when following a difficult break up with a girlfriend I drunk half a bottle of gin, and half a bottle of vodka before even leaving the flat. I blame the character you know as Ross for that.

The best thing about the Student's Union was the price of drinks was always noticeably lower than the outside world, and there was always some kind of mad promotion on.

As a group we would generally follow the curve of the promotions and end up drinking whatever was on offer. I can remember them once accidentally ordering, or possibly just finding, a case of Babycham and selling the bottles for a pound a piece. These were purchased fairly exclusively by us. I liked the link with Babyshambles and Ross liked the link to cult TV show *Bottom*. Either way, it was disgusting. In my first year I can remember drinking a lot of Snakebite[1] because it was the best thing available for your money. I also remember it for the fact on the nights I was violently sick it would invariably be purple.

By the end of my second year I was drinking a concoction known as Fanta Ice, which was two shots of Vodka and a bottle of Fanta, a bargain at £2.50, plus it tasted a lot better than anything else I had been drinking. It also didn't seem to rape me quite as badly as Snakebite had been.

It should also be noted, nights out drinking Snakebite always ended in someone spilling their drink all over you, meaning you had to deal with the fact your

---

[1] A pint glass composed of equal measures of lager and cider and topped with a shot of blackcurrant cordial

cherished t-shirt from Amsterdam would never be the same again.

At the end of the day these were all just passing fancies, and as anyone who knows me properly will tell you, my drink is Jack Daniel's. I had a count through the stories and believe the majority at least mention it, if it isn't being explicitly drunk by a character who is essentially me. I know people who say they have drunk so much Jack they have sworn themselves off it. They say they can no longer stand the smell, but I have been off my face on whiskey more times than I care to remember and I just keep crawling back like an abused spouse.

The funny thing is I only started drinking Jack Daniel's when I was really into the Rat Pack, and that was all they ever seemed to be drinking. I don't think I was even aware of how it was perceived as being a cool thing to drink by everyone else as well. I just wanted to be propped against the bar with Frank, Sammy and Dean.

Every birthday and Christmas I would be guaranteed a big bottle as a present, and these would last for a good few weeks of term, where I was happy to be drinking something I enjoyed.

Every term I returned home I seemed to do so with more stuff, more material items, and this could only be put down to one issue, I was buying a lot more.

I could never call myself materialistic or superficial because I have seen those people and I could never be that way, but the fact is while I was at university I did have an invested interest in *stuff*. I wanted to just have things. I would like to think the majority were items that could serve me a purpose, or had a use and I hadn't been completely indoctrinated into consumerism, but who really needs that many DVD boxsets?

I just checked the state of my shelves now and it bothers me I have bought so many films, and most of them were bought with my student loan or with wages I earned during the holidays.

There was never any question with buying things in the first couple of years. I would just order whatever I wanted. I signed up for a Play and Amazon account early on and the idea I could click a button and all of this stuff would just appear inside our front door was amazing to me. I think a lot of the problem is I just love receiving post. I think there is something inherently good in it. I'm still waiting on my Hogwarts acceptance letter.

Another important thing to remember is my years at university were an exciting time for music, particularly British rock music. I may just be rose tinting it or it may just be my heyday. I would scour record stores for new music, read *NME* religiously and even made an attempt at DJing. The majority of music I listen to now is either of the 60's and 70's, as a result of a childhood with glam rock loving parents, or from 2002-2008, the period in which I finished school up until when I graduated from university.

During that time I got completely lost in music. It was like a drug for me, and I made a lot of friends for life during the time as a result of our mutual love for music and our disdain for having to be bullied over it to start with. How interesting it was how quickly everything we had been shoulder barged for in the corridors at school suddenly became acceptable and cool as soon as it was played on Radio One, and available on t-shirts in Topshop.

Those years were great for music. There was the whole guitar-based indie revival thing and I rode that wave all the way in. I would spend my Saturday nights fist-pumping and twizzling about to The Futureheads, Franz Ferdinand, The Bravery, The Strokes, The Libertines, The Cribs, Cajun Dance Party, Arctic Monkeys, Kaiser Chiefs. I loved them all, and for the most part I still do.

I instantly judge people based on what music they listen to, and no, there is nothing wrong with that. It is scientifically proven people who listen to rock 'n' roll have a much higher chance of not being a complete cunt.

The idea of downloading music was just a threat at the time. I didn't have an iPod until I finished my first year so up until then I was carting around a Walkman and about eight batteries just to go to a lecture. I downloaded a bit but for the most part it was just to have compilation CDs and stuff, probably to try and impress girls.

I can remember buying a lot of music during my time at uni, both new bands and some cool stuff I had missed the first time round like Patti Smith and Van Morrison. There was always music for me. Even as I write this I have to have something on in the background. It is similar to how a homeowner will leave the TV or radio on so their cat or dog doesn't feel lonely.

In terms of other entertainment we had to make do with what the seasons would allow. Our campus was desolate at times. If you didn't have a car there was really nowhere else for you to go, unless you could deal with the hassle of getting a bus or a lift. I would literally spend weeks without leaving campus. I probably went a little stir crazy in that time.

We ended up finding the most bizarre things to amuse ourselves. I think we all regressed a little as well. In the Spring we would collect daffodils and climb trees and get chased by badgers. In the Summer we would have barbeques and play guitar out on the lawn, and run around the grounds causing havoc. In the Autumn we would play conkers and football. In the Winter we would build igloos and drink cocoa and have snowball fights and complain the heating never seemed to be working in our flats. Those kind of things can keep you amused for the seasons. There was one day when *Harry* and I set up a number of booby traps down the hallway for our long-suffering flatmates to return to after lectures. These mostly involved tripwires, water balloons and flour. The wooden banister in one particular flat was ruined with the swelling of contained water. The walls would flake away where the plaster was soaked through, but we ran the place into the ground for our own amusement. It was our playground.

The next point to address is clothes.

It's probably the next in order of importance anyway. I don't think I went completely overboard whilst I was at university in terms of purchasing clothes. I know I really got into charity shops, especially where costumes were concerned for nights out. I didn't really have an alternative. I would buy shirts and jumpers from charity shops, as well as anything else I found I thought was cool and would make my room seem more like a bohemian palace of wonder. I was, and still am, of the belief what we wear says a lot about us, so I wore a lot of band t-shirts and a lot of stripes, and that really hasn't changed. As I write this I am actually wearing a t-shirt I bought from Spitalfields market during that time.

I would save up my pennies and head into London to buy a lot of t-shirts from Camden or other trendy areas, and then they would shrink after one wash because I insisted on tumble drying absolutely everything rather than trying to find somewhere to hang it.

The t-shirts I bought that just about covered my goods would then sit at bellybutton level and I would deliberate over wearing them for a good few days afterwards before throwing them out. It's just another example of how incredibly wasteful I was at the time.

Studying law meant at the start of each year I was supposed to spend between a hundred and two hundred pounds on the key books that would be covered. The only time I can remember actually doing so was in the second year, and I made very little use of them. They are still under my bed today. The majority of my work I would try and do using the outdated books in the library and the Internet. It wasn't the best way of working but I have never really been one for making things easy for myself. As far as I was concerned the loan into my account each term was for drink and good times, and I wasn't going to mess about using it to buy books. If I did it would be the works of Murakami or Easton Ellis, not textbooks.

I think that is about all I have to say on the subject. It was a period of my life that really made me question exactly what we do with our money. I went without it for the longest time, so when I graduated and got a job I just started spending it all, thinking that was what we were all supposed to do, as though it was what was expected of us. The more I earned the more I spent, and sometimes I would spend more than I earned, and I would shrug it off because there was always more money coming in and I had always experienced a lot worse.

The problem is none of it really adds anything to what we do. There are very few things I have paid out for I think were truly worth it. I've got to a point where I have enough things. It's rare I am moved so far as to buy anything beyond my amenities. I have my books, and I have my music and there is little outside of that. I would rather use money for experiences, to be able to go off and do things, or to put it somewhere safe towards the house I one day intend on buying and filling with memories. That seems a lot more important to me.

What I think I am saying is the place all the money went, the answer to my question, or *the* question, because technically I can't really claim it as mine when I stole it from the lyrics to *What A Waster* by The Libertines is, it went on getting me to this point, to realising I am fine as I am, and I want to write for a living, and it taught me a thousand other lessons, and it caught me some fantastic friends, and some silly memories I'm trying to turn into stories, and it was all worthwhile.

I Now Pronounce You

MICHAEL
July 2011

As I climbed up from the depths of London's underground system I tried to work out how long it had been since we had all been together. I had spoken to Oliver every day but Eli and Ross were a different story altogether. I didn't know what they were doing or who they were doing or where they were living but assumed they were still living at home because it made me feel better about my lot in life, or what I considered to be my lot when obviously it was all my own decision and my own doing.

It was an unusually summery Summer's day. I couldn't have fathomed it back in February, when I had first received the invitation that had brought us back together, the wedding of our old university friend Lisa and the boyfriend it seemed to me she had only just met.

I had been reliably informed it had been two years. I had met him once or twice, notably on a night out in Camden for Lisa's birthday where he won me over completely by matching me drink for drink on Jack Daniel's and for then paying for a number of shots of Tequila for us both. If a dude buys me a drink on our first meeting then he can do little wrong from that point onwards, which is quite a good rule for life.

I got to the top of the winding staircase and out into the air, hoping it would be cooler than the stuffy trains. I was out of luck.

The humidity of London's streets was an exact parallel of the underground and I knew there would be no relief. I took one headphone out of my ear where it had been pumping *Romance At Short Notice* into my brain. I pulled my iPhone from my pocket and called Oliver. He answered almost immediately.

'Why aren't you in me yet?!'
'Are you drunk?' I replied.
'Getting there. Hurry up, we're going to be late'.
'I'm here. You told me to get to Tottenham Court Road'.
'Yeah, we're here'.

I wandered back and forth across the exit of the tube station. I didn't really want to play games. I needed a drink.

'I can see you' he said, 'take a step to your left'.

I looked ahead, round the side of a kiosk selling tacky London shit. I could make out Oliver, stood just outside a pub with a beer in his hand and a quiff in his hair. I grinned and dashed over to him.

Sat behind him, trying to juggle a bottle of cider, a glass of ice, a packet of cigarettes and a lighter, was Eli. Ross was nowhere to be seen.

'Where's Ross?' I asked, finally remembering to hang up the call I was conducting with the person stood immediately to my left.
'He isn't invited to the service' said Eli, still sat on the stoop outside the pub.
'Why?'
'Why do you think?'
'Ahh, I see'.
'He's coming with Danny later'.
'Have you got them anything?' Oliver asked.
'No. Should I?'

Eli finally stopped fiddling about with his trinkets and stood up, almost reaching the height of our nipples.

'Alright fella, long time no see' he said, and launched at me in a hug. I liked the fact there was absolutely no animosity between us over the fact we had not kept in touch, or attempted contact for the best part of a year. We could just fit back into our roles and steam ahead.

'Didn't you have time to do your hair' he asked.

'Very funny' I said, self-consciously sweeping my fringe from my eyes.

'Nah, you're looking sharp mate' he grinned.

'Thanks, so are you. I like the tie clip'.

'Yeah, it's gold. My mum got it for me'.

'Oh yeah? How is Vicky?'

'Leave it out…I'm joking mate, she's very happy'.

'That's good to hear. What are you up to these days?'

'I'm still at the bed store. What about you? Working up in the city right?'

'Yeah, I am. It's not too bad'.

'That's good mate. I'm glad you're doing alright'.

'Have I got time to grab a pint or are we moving on?'

'You've got time'.

'Right, do either of you want anything?'

'I'll have another cider' said Eli.

'You greedy little bear, you've just got one' said Oliver, feigning surprise.

I headed inside to get a drink.

It was only as I stepped back outside I realised it was only half past eleven, and I hadn't had a pint at that time in three years. I also realised when I had last drunk at the same time it had been with the same people. I had been off my face before teatime then. I hoped the same wouldn't take place. I was still a danger to myself when drunk.

With the first pint sunk we headed on, trying to work out where we could go to buy a last minute wedding present, and whether we could get it gift wrapped to save us the embarrassment of presenting it to the happy couple in a plastic bag.

As we made our way out into the human traffic of Oxford Street we headed for the big department stores, stopping only so Oliver could hand all his change over to a homeless man trying to offer out copies of the *Big Issue*.

Once inside we were stuck with the dilemma of exactly what to get them, and spent about twenty minutes riding on escalators in a montage of confusion.

'Can we get them pillows?' asked Eli.

'You can't buy a couple pillows' scoffed Oliver.

'Yeah, Lisa already has a pretty good pair'.

'What about a lamp?' I asked.

'I love lamp!' screamed Oliver, loud enough for shopping couples to turn at us, disgusted.

'Well, what should we get them then?'

'A decanter?'

'A fountain pen?'

'Whiskey tumblers?'

'Yes!'

'What?'

'The whiskey glasses!'

'Yeah, we could get those and a nice bottle, and we are done!'

It was nice we could still come to a conclusion together, make a consensus and finally have a plan of action.

Eli and I were happy to leave the rest of the business to Oliver, completing the actual purchase on his card, (so we could pay him our share in cash later) and getting it giftwrapped. We all competed to write the funniest message in the card we attached to the perfectly wrapped present and then we were ready to head off to the wedding.

'Have you boys eaten anything yet?'

'It would be a good idea before we drink anymore. I don't know if there will be food later on'.

Oliver waved his hand out towards the road and instantly summoned a black cab.

'Marylebone Town Hall please mate'.

I was instantly taken back to nights out at uni but was drawn to the scrolling streets of London. I felt like the ultimate tourist. Sometimes it is very easy to forget how beautiful London can be, and all it contains, and can offer.

The cab pulled up outside the impressive structure and I realised why Lisa had chosen it as the venue for her wedding service. I was also impressed her fiancé Max had agreed to go along with it.

Marylebone Town Hall was the chosen venue for the wedding of Paul and Linda McCartney as well as for Chrissie Hynde, John Hurt and Antonio Banderas. Not that they married one another, but have at one point or another got married there. It was really cool.

'We've got time. We can just wander about until we find a greasy little *caff* somewhere' said Eli, thinking with his belly and not pronouncing café properly.

'Yeah alright, I need to eat'.

We wandered about five minutes down the road before we came across the perfect place, a tiny eatery with Formica-topped tables, and ketchup bottles shaped like oversized plastic tomatoes. It was a level we were comfortable with. It reminded me of Flames, our old haunt near campus.

We all ordered burgers, in varying forms, and then sat watching the clock and shooting the shit until the food came.

'You still with your bird?' asked Eli.

'Yeah, I am' I replied, deciding not to correct him for using the term 'bird', a move I definitely would have made if my *bird* had been present.

'How's it going?' he asked.

'Really good thanks' I replied, pulling the ring pull back on a can of Diet Coke.

'What about you?' I asked.

'You know me, always got my eye on the hunnies' he replied. I decided not to question it any further.

'Still playing bowls?'

'Yeah, got the regionals next week'.

The conversation stopped dead for two reasons. The first being I have absolutely no idea how bowls works. All I do know, or all Eli has taught me, is if you ask anyone who plays lawn bowls if it is basically the same as boule, which we have all played on holiday, they get highly agitated.

The second reason was our food arrived and we were distracted with the rituals of dousing our food in our chosen condiments. Eli was one for drowning everything at his disposal in vinegar so we all had to suffer the pungent, acidic smell as we tried to put away the food which served us one single purpose, to line our stomachs before we started drinking.

Oliver liked to take his time preparing his food. It was like watching a ballet, accompanied by ketchup.

There was no time for conversation, just the sound of bent-pronged forks being jammed into chipped plates, of aluminium cans clanking against teeth, and then with the smacking of lips and the clanging of cutlery onto empty plates we were done.

With full bellies and the bill paid we headed back out into the sunshine to make sure we were at the hall before the bride arrived, as is the custom. It was probably for the best we ate as quickly as we did because within minutes of us arriving outside, and shaking hands with Lisa's brother and dad, she wandered around the corner in the reddest dress I have ever seen.

To be honest I don't know why I expected anything different, Lisa is hardly one to follow protocol and of course it extended to undoing the traditions of a wedding. I couldn't even describe it as being confrontational, regardless of the fact she once dressed up on Halloween as Lady Di.

It is literally just the way she is, and it's one of her many endearing characteristics. She doesn't take any shit from anyone, and during our time together at university I would often be protected by her caring wing.

She looked absolutely amazing though, in a fitted, strapped dress, with her hair more platinum blonde than I could ever remember seeing it, carefully curled up and held back on one side by a giant red flower. I think Oliver even wolf whistled at her. It was also typical of her to walk, tottering slightly on heels that looked like they would carve her feet clean off before the day was through. Lisa wasn't one for the pretense of arriving in a limo or any other kind of fanciful vehicle. She was too grounded for such things, and too independent to be driven about.

'We should probably get inside' I said, 'I don't think we're supposed to walk in at the same time as the bride'.

'Yeah, don't want to draw all the attention' said Eli with a cheeky wink. I couldn't say if he was joking. Oliver's phone started ringing. There was a hurried exchange, of which we could hear half clearly, and the other half remained distorted and swirling like a *Peanuts* sketch.

'Alright Dal'
'...'
'What do you mean?'
'...'
'Well, where are you?'
'...'
'Yeah, it's just down the road'.
'...'
'On the right'.
'...'
'Which direction are you facing?'
'...'
'So you're just outside the station?'
'...'
'Can you see the café on the corner, with the yellow sign?'
'...'
'Well where are you then?'
'...'
'No Dal, it's about to start'.
'...'
'For fuck's sake, stay there!'
He hung up with a stab of his thumb.

'What's happening?' I asked.

'Dal reckons he is lost. I'll be back in a minute'.
He started at pace off down the street.

'Bet they both miss it' said Eli as we slowly made our way inside.

We were ushered down the hall, up some stairs and into a room of about thirty people, including a number of faces I recognised from university or from photos Lisa had previously shown me of her nearest and dearest.

Trying to draw as little attention to ourselves as possible we made our way to the back of the room, because every single seat was taken. I quickly propped myself up against the wall, by the window, to absorb the small amount of breeze floating in.

Before the ceremony began, the registrar walked towards me, reached around my side, and pulled the window shut tight.

'Gets a bit distracting with the traffic' he explained. I didn't give a shit. I was going to sweat through my suit.

Lisa was walked in by her dad, who looked happier and prouder than I had ever seen him. The room gave a collective gasp because it was such a beautiful moment, and fitted her personality perfectly. Max stood up and everything was right in the world. I could hear music, I could see doves and love hearts floating around the room.

Oliver and Dal chose this wonderful and pure moment to barge into the room looking flustered. They had Lisa's friend Padmini in tow.

'Sorry...sorry...sorry' they repeated as they tried to duck down out of the way and head towards the back, treading on toes, and elbowing people in the head. They slowly drew the attention in an arc across the room, towards me, making me embarrassed, when I had done nothing wrong except by association, as usual.

'Fucking hell, I'm knackered' said Dal, leaning against the now closed window. He wouldn't offer me a friendly 'hello' until after the ceremony. I just had to slide along the space I had carefully reserved for myself by the window ledge to make room for him. I could see the beads of sweat on his thick brow.

The registrar stood and addressed the room. We all stood with him.

'You join us today to celebrate the wedding of Max and Lisa…'

I've only been to a few weddings, but it was one of the most intimate and beautiful occasions of my life. It felt like we were really part of it. I felt honoured to be there and it was only then it dawned on me exactly what was happening and what it all meant. Lisa was the second of my university friends to get married, a sign of more to come no doubt, and an example of how it can really happen to anyone.

Lisa was the first friend I made on campus. The first person it felt who had taken the time to talk to me, beyond my flatmates who were obliged to, because they were lumbered with me for a year.

Lisa came and sat with me outside the bar on our first night on campus and I will never forget it. I had been characteristically sick and was trying to get some fresh air when we were forced into conversation after someone else realised we were both from Essex.

Lisa had always been quite vocal about her views on marriage, but I saw before my eyes what happens to people when they fall in love and it was a complete change and a complete joy.

It was all over so quickly and then we were stood on the stairs outside, confetti in hand, ready to meet the married couple, every girl with black lines running down their cheeks and every boy with a look of 'you poor daft bastard' in their eyes.

As they made it to the bottom of the stairs a rickshaw arrived, decorated in pink crepe banners and roses. They got in and headed off for Embankment, where the reception was due to take place. The crowd slowly dispersed, heading for the Tube or reaching out for cabs.

As for us it was time to get some drink in our bellies before taking to the hired boat, which would ferry us up and down the Thames for the duration of the evening. We got into a waiting cab and headed down to the river. We still had time to kill before the happy couple arrived, because there is only so fast a rickshaw can move, so we joined those who were only invited to the evening event in the Australian themed pub facing the estuary.

We were in the pub when I first caught sight of Ross. It had easily been a year since I had seen him, possibly even two and yet the way he spoke and everything else about him was a reminder of the time we had spent together at university. There were no revered moments of wisdom or lessons learned with Ross like there were with the others, he was just as reckless and just as lost and there was almost something admirable in it despite it meaning he would still be a nightmare with a couple of drinks inside him.

'Get us a drink then Michael' he said to me, because some things will just never change.
'Why?' I asked.
'Come on Michael, me thirsty, me so thirsty'.
All the old irritations came crawling out of him in one sentence.
'Alright, let's get a beer'.
We headed off to the bar and before long were gathered around with Eli, Oliver, Danny, Sophie, Abbie and an assortment of other characters.
It was like another night gathered together in the bar, or in someone's kitchen, or out in the gardens of the Manor House on campus. It was just the way we all felt comfortable, and things kicked right back in. I shook hands, and I hugged, and I told people the same things

about what I was doing, and I told the same jokes over and over, and there were no holds barred.

'How's things then Michael?' asked Danny, who I had found myself beside.
'Yeah, pretty good actually'.
'You still playing guitar?'
'Yeah', I said, 'of course. What about you?'
'Yeah, I try to. It's hard with work and that, it's hard to find time'.
'Yeah, I understand' I said, despite the fact I didn't, because I will always make time for guitar.
'How's your girlfriend? You still with her' he asked, which was odd because I knew I hadn't seen him since I had started dating her. I quickly realised it was the wonders of social networking keeping us involved in one another's lives. It was a blessing and a curse at the same time. It meant you could check up on one another in a positive way but it also felt you didn't need to be physically present to communicate.

Weeks, months, years had passed since we had all been together. I wondered how long it would be before it could happen again this completely.
'Yeah, very happy' I said.
'You still with yours?'
'Yes mate, very happy, he said, echoing my own sentiment.
We both sipped from our pints, collecting our thoughts for a moment.

'Guys, the boat is ready to leave' someone said, propping themselves up on the leather sofa and staring out one of the dirty porthole windows of the pub.

Everyone went to stand at once, but didn't move on. There was a collective gasp as we all up-ended our glasses and sunk whatever we had left of our drinks. I watched the ceiling lights dazzle and disperse through the thick spun glass as I cleared my pint.

With sloppy lips and wet eyes we ran out, across four lanes of traffic, and up the stairs towards the gangway. The boat was hooting a final warning, it was ready to depart.

We were all waving our hands over our heads, trying to stop the last section; the plank, from being lifted up and back, into the door of the ship and heading off without us. All I could hear was the tottering of heels on the slatted slope.

Oliver held back and let everyone run on ahead of him, trying to headcount and make sure we were all present and correct. He grabbed Sophie who had the highest of heels on, and was therefore the furthest back, and charged her forwards.

It was too late though. As soon as we were on board they lifted the plank and we started drifting away from the dock. Oliver and Sophie grinded to a halt on the precipice of what had become a pier.

We all rushed up the stairs inside to watch the action, collecting along the railing above the doorway to see what would happen.

'You'll have to wait until we turn back' called one of the ship's staff, holding the gangplank aloft in the doorway. Oliver started to take his jacket off. Everyone on the boat looked at each other. He handed it across to Sophie. I noticed he was in a waistcoat, the pretentious fuck.

'Fine', he said, 'I'll just jump onboard'.

We weren't sure what was going to happen. From where we were stood, above it all, it looked like a reasonable distance, heading on for five feet. From a stand I didn't know if he would make it. There was a moment of deliberation. The gap increased to five and a half feet'.

'If I don't make it, you're coming in after me' he said, pointing at the staff, threatening.

He began swinging his arms in long, exaggerated movements, like he was warming up to leap the now six-foot gap between his toes and his proposed landing point. He made his last minute preparations and I couldn't help but hope he would actually go for it, regardless of the outcome. It would be what he always wanted, it would be an anecdote.

'Jump!' we all shouted in unison, and it was the turning point. They couldn't have a wedding attendee slamming his face against the side of the boat and disappearing into the grimy depths of the river.

'Woah, stay there, don't jump. We'll get you on'.

He signaled to someone who signaled to whoever else and the boat started drifting back towards the dock.

We let out a collective cheer and Oliver waved his fists in the air in a moment of triumph against 'the man' before allowing Sophie to step aboard before himself.

The boat set off again, pulling away successfully this time and heading out to sea, or at least river, while we wandered around trying to work out where things were, what we could get away with as the day stretched out into our evening, and most importantly, the location of the bar.

The upper deck of the boat was half bar and dance floor area, at the bow, and half open top balcony, at the stern. We headed for the back and stood around in tight little circles to smoke for the majority of the evening.

Once everyone had drinks in one hand and cigarettes in the other, they decided to announce the speeches. I chose the moment to catch up with Nate and Carp who I wasn't expecting to see at all. They had lived in the flat beneath and across from me in my final year, when if anything I was most isolated and insane. For some reason they thought I was cool and would often invite me downstairs to play *Guitar Hero* and smoke weed with them.

'What are you doing now?' I asked.

'Well, I graduated last Summer' said Nate, 'and now I work in mobile marketing'.

I didn't know what mobile marketing was, but didn't want to raise the point.

'What are you up to?' Carp asked me, 'still working up here?'

He swung his head around, indicating to the passing sides of the river.

'Yeah, it's not too far from here actually, I'll point it out as we go past, it's right by the Tate Modern'.

'Oh good, I look forward to it' said Carp sarcastically, and walked off to make conversation with someone else. I could feel our moment together had passed, in the way a lot of my friendships from university had expired. Some of the people I called friends I did so purely down to geographical closeness rather than any real bond between us. If we had met in the outside world, under different circumstances, we would not have gelled, or would have walked off in completely different directions shortly after.

It didn't hurt as much as I thought it might. It was quite a comfortable sensation. I had the people I needed.

I shifted towards the steel railing, which ran around the open stern where Oliver was leaning with eyes narrowed like Shatner, staring out at the white line we were cutting in the murky water. The sun was just entering the last quarter of the sky, and as we rolled along it was partially masked by high-rise office blocks and other city features.

Oliver lifted a cigarette to his mouth and then blew the smoke out melodramatically before addressing me.

'You know, I've noticed you around' he said in mock seduction.

'Fuck off' I laughed.

'Did you see me freak the boat people out?'

'I don't think they are called boat people Oli'.

'The *navy* then. Did you see their stupid faces?'

'Were you really going to jump?' I asked.

'Fuck no, I don't want AIDS from that water!' he replied, flicking his cigarette into it.

'Have you not already got it then?'

'No'.

'Oh right, you don't know. Look, I went to get tested and-'.

He laughed in the way only Oliver could laugh at my attempts at jokes.

'The baby is mine?' he added. Our sense of humour is a hard thing to explain, without looking like we should be locked up. Just because we joke about those subjects doesn't mean we don't respect or fear them, it just means we are beyond excluding it. Nothing is sacred. There is no safe ground.

London continued to trail behind us, judging.

The speeches ended with a round of applause which started inside where people could actually hear what was being said, and titter at the jokes, and ended with Oliver and I issuing a couple of claps apiece.

We watched between other people's heads as the couple revolved and dipped to their first dance as husband and wife. In traditional Lisa and Max style it was nothing ordinary, *Baby, I Love You* by The Ramones.

Afterwards they gave way for others to join in and one by one people filtered onto the laminated area. With the ceiling standing at just under seven foot it was like kettling. Oliver and I headed straight through for the bar. I had already reached my beer limit, the point at which I realise I am too full of foam, and switched over to Jack Daniel's. It was what I knew best and what I was comfortable with, which is another general rule for life.

It was then the band took to the stage.

We stood perched against the bar, which was just wide enough for two people to stand either in front of or behind, and watched the absolute horrors we called friends as they pranced up and down parodying the genuine couples, pretending they could foxtrot or tango or whatever else they fancied.

It would have been embarrassing if it was anywhere else but there was a sense we had been invited to serve as some sort of entertainment for the other guests. It was made all the better by the fact the band were so good. Max worked as a guitar tech by day, both at a school and through private tuition but he also filled his boots by playing in a number of bands, I believe at one point there were seven on the go. It meant when it came to entertainment for his wedding he had the pick of the bunch, and those chosen were part of his reggae outfit.

It didn't matter what they played because we stuck right with them. Oliver and I downed our drinks and joined the others on the dance floor. Oliver was just able to swing back and forth without making contact with the ceiling, he was the tallest of us. It was like the best of the old times, when we would completely disregard everything else that was going on and just get caught up in trying to make each other laugh. Danny was swishing his hips around, trying to disguise the fact he was in fact an incredibly smooth dancer. Eli was pogoing, and trying to balance a pint, while screaming obscenities at the band. I was performing my only and awkward dance moves like an eighties dad. Ross held up his near-full pint in the centre of the group.

'Someone watch this, I'm going for a slash' he said, and handed the pint to Eli who instinctively took a deep gulp of it as soon as Ross was out of sight.

'Hold it steady' said Oliver, 'I'm dipping my old chap in there'.

For some reason we didn't stop him, it seemed like a perfectly reasonable and hilarious thing to do when your friend foolishly let his guard down and decided to trust you. Oliver stood shoulder-to-shoulder with Eli and I, unleashing the beast right there, as the band played *Don't Stand So Close To Me*.

'Fuck that's cold' he said as he shook off and returned his weapon to his suit trousers. We weren't going to say anything, we were getting enough of a kick the way things were going. Ross returned and we laughed each time his lips met with the plastic rim of the glass. Oliver tried to usher him along by getting him to down it but Ross refused outright, assuming something must have been awry. It was funny anyway.

Once we had exhausted our raisin lungs dancing like fools we headed back outside and joined some of the other guests in smoking a joint off the stern. The whole time we were worried we were going to be clocked by a member of the boat's crew and made to walk the plank. We needn't have feared, they seemed to have hidden themselves away soon after our departure. We were obviously a little more out of hand than what they were used to on their river cruises.

I started to get hungry again and thought there was very little I could do about it until we docked and located a kebab house. It didn't stop me from complaining though. The weed had hit me and mixed with the unusually high amount of alcohol I had managed to imbibe. I was deep down pleased with myself, and my grin showed it.

I was fine in fact, until Ross came up alongside me with a paper plate of buffet food.

'Woah, where did you get that?!' I screamed. Eli and Oliver turned round.

'There's food downstairs' said Ross, and before he could say anymore the three of us had dashed off, cramming our suited shoulders down the narrow winding stairwell and then scanning the lower deck of the boat.

There was a room underneath the dance floor where a table had been put aside for food. We had definitely not been made aware of it, unless it was mentioned as part of the speeches we couldn't hear because we had been outside smoking.

We piled plates up with everything we could and then took to a corner to avoid anyone upstairs becoming aware there was food available. It had become our treasure, our precious, and we had to do everything possible to keep it to ourselves. After clearing another plate each we ran upstairs to try and make our mutual disappearance seem as brief and coincidental as possible.

'Where have you guys been?' asked Sophie.

'Nowhere' Oliver said quickly, and led us through to the bar. Along the way I noticed Nate dancing with a couple of children he had procured from somewhere. They were laughing at him as he hid behind a giant red helium balloon.

'Alright darling' Oliver said to the barmaid, 'three Fosters please'.

'No Oliver, I can't drink anymore beer'.

'Oh right, sorry. Two beers and one Jack and coke please'.

'Are you not getting one for Ross?' Eli asked.

'No, look at him' Oliver said, pointing out to the centre of the dance floor where Ross stood alone, jigging a quarter pint of flat beer in a plastic cup back and forth and pretending he knew the words to *Red, Red Wine*.

'Oh god, that's embarrassing' said Eli, 'he reminds me of my aunt'.

'If she's anything like your mum I'd still fuck her' said Oliver.

We stood and continued to watch Ross. He seemed pretty oblivious of the three pairs of eyes on him. He seemed completely oblivious of everything in fact. It was hard to work out exactly what he was doing or thinking, but then his mouth dropped open and he proceeded to vomit into his pint glass. There was nothing we could have done. It was such an immediate thing and we literally had no time to react, let alone stop him. It was like a deer running out in front of a car. Ross looked around, and thinking nobody had noticed, precariously balanced the now full pint glass on one of the speakers the band were using.

'Fuck, I can't let him carry on like that' said Oliver, darting forward and resuming the father role he had long ago taken over Ross. I was reminded of what he had said to me about Ross when we had first met – "sort of a friend, but someone you feel obliged to look after". The relationship hadn't just died away because we graduated. Oliver had to keep it going whenever the pair of them were together, and it was for that specific reason he had limited Ross's access to his life since they had left campus.

I watched as Oliver attempted to slap Ross in the face and knock a bit of sense into him. Ross took this as a queue to rest his chin on his chest and vomit down his shirt. He then wiped his mouth with the back of his hand and gave Oliver a look that said *I've just been sick down myself, and there is absolutely nothing constructive I am going to do about it.*

As this point Lisa came rushing over, somehow immediately aware one of the guests at her wedding was being sick on themselves and the dance floor. We all suddenly became aware of why it was Ross had only been invited to the evening event.

The music suddenly cut out as the bassist, who had up until then been doing his upmost best to ignore what was happening, and was bopping up and down a foot away from where someone was vomiting on the floor, knocked the full pint of sick backwards onto the keyboardist who jumped up, pulling the cables from the outlet in the wall.

'-fucking sort him out' Lisa could then be heard to be screaming across the entire boat. Oliver grabbed Ross by the shoulders and marched him down the stairs and into the toilets. The band scrabbled about on the floor to try and plug their instruments back in, and Lisa was left laying kitchen roll over a pile of sick on a dance floor on the day of her wedding.

Eli and I remained pinned to the bar, sure we must have been completely invisible, blending into our natural environment. It didn't work.

'Michael, can you sort this out' Lisa asked, and threw the kitchen roll at me. By the time I looked up from the bundle of paper thrown into my arms she was walking back out to the deck and lighting a cigarette. When I turned, Eli had managed to disappear completely. I hiked up the bottom of my suit trousers and bent down to sweep up the sick and tissue. The band started playing *Valerie*.

Once I was done I headed back downstairs to wash my hands. As I tried to open the door it stopped, catching against Oliver's back as he stood leant over Ross who continued to gurgle into the toilet bowl. The bathroom was clearly not intended for three, and I had to squeeze myself in and then push the door shut again to give us some kind of privacy.

'I can't believe him' said Oliver, looking up at me and simultaneously rubbing Ross's back like an overzealous father to be. 'I mean, I expect it from you, but we all do, *you're* the lightweight'. I couldn't dispute it.

'I didn't think he had that much' I said.

'He didn't! I don't know what his problem is, just showing off probably'.

'What do you want to do?' I asked him.

'Well I can't fucking leave him. It's like he can't do anything without dragging me down with him, it fucks me off. There are bridesmaids up there going wanting'.

Oliver made an excellent point. Ross always seemed to implode and suck us into the black hole with him, just because we were in orbit. There was no way we could or should be responsible for him. There was no way I would expect anyone to look after me in the same way if it had been me doubled over the bowl. I would always run off and take care of it myself, because I would be ashamed. Ross just didn't seem to have the same settings, he wasn't capable of understanding, like a Vulcan, or a naughty puppy. It didn't matter how many times you smacked him on the nose he would continue to piss on the rug and expect you to leave dinner in his bowl.

Eventually Oliver and I just gave up on him, in the way people always seem to have to if they want to get out alive. We made it back upstairs and the band were just winding up into the last couple of songs and we could see Embankment lit up in the darkness, because it was after pub closing. We knew we had to finish off big, like pyrotechnics at the end of the show.

We all collected in a circle and struck a groove and when the band finished and we had pulled into the dock we still weren't satisfied, we weren't ready to get off, despite the fact we had been warned we had to be off before midnight or there would be additional charges.

It didn't matter to us in the slightest, a fact proven by the way Lisa took to the decks and played a couple of choice songs to finish it all starting with *Come On Eileen*, to push us over the edge and send us spiraling out for the night, like a cliff face giving way under it's own weight and plummeting into the sea below.

Ross chose this moment to stumble back up from the toilets, and try to dance with us. He smelt like Wotsits and sick, and there was a dark patch on his shirt where he had tried to dab the mess out with balled up tissue paper.

When *Hey Jude* started I knew it was the end though, because Hey Jude is always and should always be the last song, nothing can follow it. It's the kind of song people end up repeating over and over on the way out of a party, and Lisa knew that.

In her infinite wisdom as a Student's Union and private hire DJ she knew if you want people to join arms and forces, and see out the night then you play Hey Jude. So with raised hands we bashed along to the beat of the song and screamed the lyrics at each other. There were fifty raised voices, and there were arms around shoulders like warriors, and suit jackets were swung around and disregarded on the benches at the side, and the whole time we continued to stamp our feet on the laminate and pummel our fists into the ceiling of the little boat in the dock.

When the music cut out, along with the engine, there was still a mighty chorus of people singing '*Na, na na na-na-na-na*' which just couldn't be silenced. It was an incredible moment and an amazing end to the night.

The door behind the bar opened and the captain of our ship looked out to see what was going to happen. He tried to call for someone to stop what we were doing, but it was as unavoidable as the tides, and soon the chorus of voices turned from The Beatles classic to a simple but similarly catchy line:

'Sink the boat! Sink the boat! Sink the boat!'

We stomped harder and we punched harder and as the boat sat in the dock people up on the bankside looked over, trying to work out what the hell could have been going on, and we laughed and threatened to take down the crew with us, and we saluted and swung around each other with locked elbows. It was only when Lisa laid down the law and told us to stop that it all subsided.

We went out the back once more, for our last cigarette on the balcony, looking out at the twinkling light pollution reflected in the Thames.

As I stood enjoying the last cigarette I ever wanted, Dal came at me like a pirate.

'Come here, you fucking-' he said, and swung his arms around me, dropping what I am quite sure would have been something anti-Semitic from the end of his outburst. It was like being hit by a missile. Padmini stood behind him laughing, obviously not realising I was in mortal peril. There was an imminent threat of a snog rape taking place. Dal hadn't *got* me in quite some time.

The only time I could recall being captured with any clarity was one night after a Law Society dinner when

Zach and I stole a bottle of red wine and were hiding out the back of the Manor House in a little potting shed, smoking a joint. Dal had found me and got me then, but it was the only solid memory. He had a habit of it. You put enough whiskey inside the boy and he would kiss the barnacles off the boat.

'Woah there, that's enough'.

'But I love you, you fucking –'.

Again, his utterance was lost in his lunge.

'Padmini!' I screamed, 'can you just grab him'.

She didn't though, she was busy holding her clutch bag, and laughing. I guess it you weren't me it would have looked quite funny.

'Dal, I'm going home, I've got to go' I said, and finally managed to get free of his clutches, slipping backwards and inside again, throwing my butt out to sea just before it was too late.

I hugged everyone in sight.

We made promises to meet up more often.

We said so many things, which would be lost before the morning.

I kissed Lisa, and I told her how beautiful she was, and then I stumbled off into the night with a bridesmaid in tow.

Paul Schiernecker is a writer and musician from Rayleigh, Essex. He studied Law at Buckinghamshire New University and scraped a degree.
His aim is to one day not have to answer to anyone but himself.

www.PaulSchiernecker.com

Special thanks:

Kate. Simon. Tracey. Robb. Edd. Antony. Lucy. Ashley. Jonny. Scot. Ben. Will. Chloe. Toby. Marc. Ravi. Vara. Caroline. Jenny. Wes. Katie. Michael. Cassie. Melissa. Orlagh. Kenzie. Anna. Lizzie. Mark. Tom. Dave. Pyumi. Sarah. Zara. Jack. Jamie. Tom. Sam. Claire. Colin. Jan. Mike. Fran. Adam. Stacy.

To everyone in these pages, regardless of whether you are aware of it or not.
To my family who put up with the endless tapping of keys.
To my friends who haven't seen a lot of me lately.
To my girlfriend for understanding and loving me.
To every person that ever inspired me to say or write what I think.
This is for you.

Printed in Great Britain
by Amazon.co.uk, Ltd.,
Marston Gate.